"Tom Hamblin is a true
caring, as well as a go
Along with his faithful, passi
nature Tom has a great sense of humour! His time in the
British army taught him discipline and how to persevere
in hardship. When he lived and ministered in Islamic
states he impacted many lives. Tom not only served in
countries such as Malaysia, Yemen and the Gulf States
but touched a number of other places in Asia and Africa
through his ministry among guest workers, and was
known as God's courier to the Arabian Peninsula. I can
truly say that as Tom Hamblin followed Christ, Jesus
made him a fisher of men. He has lived for God and
glorified Him through his everyday life."*

**Kamal Fahmi, Founder and International Executive
Director of Set My People Free**

*"Wherever God called him to take the Bible, Tom
responded with courage, honesty and integrity, no
matter how challenging and sensitive the country."*

**David Long, Southcote Christian Mission; Tom
Hamblin's pastor**

*"I truly believe that Tom was raised by God for such
a time as this, to bring the precious gospel to Africa.
I have witnessed how two independent prophecies to
Tom unfolded in his life; how he has met princes and
influential leaders; and how iron gates have been crushed
in inaccessible nations hostile to the gospel, in fulfilment
of the prophecies. God has taken this man, filled with
supernatural boldness, to fulfil an impossible task made
only possible by those who trust, love, and believe
Him deeply. The result of this mission impossible? An*

incredible sixteen years of Bible distribution in difficult nations, with not even a single Bible lost! And Tom Hamblin has been the man to see it through.

"I strongly recommend his book to all who are passionate about missions and who desire similar boldness to serve God. Learn from Tom as he shares his vast field experience and numerous miracles of deliverance to the glory of God!"

Pastor Jason Foo, Executive Director, His Mission, Singapore

"For over fifty years I have followed the exciting and adventurous exploits of Tom and Edna Hamblin. From our first meeting in 1964, when they were appointed as Superintendents of the Sandes Airmen's Centre at Royal Air Force Ballykelly in Northern Ireland, I knew that they were God's chosen servants to prove that God was at work building His church. I witnessed their impact on the Ballykelly base, as they enthusiastically engaged in evangelism from the Sandes Centre. Their vision that God does make a difference was an inspiration to me, together with the many service personnel and their families who were blessed by their ministry. They knew God intimately and that was their strength, as they undertook exploits for Him in the Sandes Centres in Singapore, Labuan, Kuching, and Hong Kong. However, this was to be a training ground for their activities in Borneo, as they faced various difficulties in restoring a desecrated ancient Anglican church and building two clinics in Aden, Yemen, and then spent sixteen years in the Middle East, sowing the Word of God in the language of the people – transparently, not smuggling.

"Under Their Very Eyes *is the thrilling and amazing account of what God has been doing in our day. It is a wonderfully challenging book and I recommend it as an inspirational read.*"

Squadron Leader Bob Abbott MBE

"*Tom has a depth of relationship with Christ and the fixed focus of an anointed Old Testament prophet, displayed in compassionate humanity, dependable friendship and fun.*"

John G. W. Matthews MCh., FRCS[Eng.], Consultant Surgeon[Retired]

Tom Hamblin

Acts 4 v 12/13

Deborah Meroff was a missionary journalist for thirty years and travelled to 115 countries, mostly serving with OM International. She is the author of numerous articles as well as eight other books and a blog about women and girls at risk, http://women-without-borders.net/. She now resides in Maine, USA.

Also by Deborah Meroff:

Coronation of Glory: The Story of Lady Jane Grey
Captain My Captain
Footsteps in the Sea
Riding the Storm
The Touch of the Master
True Grit: Women Taking on the World for God's Sake
Europe: Restoring Hope
Psalms from the Sea

UNDER THEIR VERY EYES

The astonishing life of Tom Hamblin,
Bible courier to Arab nations

Deborah Meroff
with Tom Hamblin

MONARCH
BOOKS

Oxford, UK, and Grand Rapids, USA

Published by Monarch Books
an imprint of
Lion Hudson plc
Wilkinson House, Jordan Hill Road,
Oxford OX2 8DR, England
Email: monarch@lionhudson.com
www.lionhudson.com/monarch

ISBN 978 0 85721 712 7
e-ISBN 978 0 85721 713 4

First edition 2016

Acknowledgments
Unless marked otherwise, Scripture quotations taken from the Holy Bible, New
International Version Anglicised. Copyright © 1979, 1984, 2011 Biblica, formerly
International Bible Society. Used by permission of Hodder & Stoughton Ltd, an
Hachette UK company. All rights reserved. "NIV" is a registered trademark of
Biblica. UK trademark number 1448790.
Scirpture quotations marked KJV taken from The Authorized (King James) Version.
Rights in the Authorized Version are vested in the Crown. Reproduced by permission
of the Crown's patentee, Cambridge University Press.

A catalogue record for this book is available from the British Library

Printed and bound in the UK, April 2016, LH26

I dedicate this book to the "treasures of darkness, riches stored in secret places". You may never be able to read this book or even know that it exists. But the Lord, your Abba Father, knows every one of you and you are precious in His sight, for you have embraced His Son, Jesus Christ (Isa) as your Saviour and Lord and you love Him with every heartbeat and fibre of your being.

You have also lived with the possibility that every day could be your last one on earth, a separation from families whom you dearly love, who will also suffer; and this causes you deep pain.

In the Word of God we are exhorted to "honour those to whom honour is due", and each memory of you moves my heart and causes me to bow humbly before our heavenly Father, in your honour. My voice lifts in thanksgiving for your faithfulness and fearlessness, even unto death. I cannot list by name the many of you whom I baptized to become followers of Christ, but I know with assurance we shall meet again in the presence of our great King Jesus!

I repeat the words of an old hymn by William Cushing that describes this wonderful day:

When He cometh, when He cometh, to make up His jewels,
All His jewels, precious jewels, His loved and His own.
He will gather, He will gather the gems for His kingdom,
All the pure ones, all the bright ones, His loved and His own.
Faithful children, faithful children, who love their Redeemer,
Are the jewels, precious jewels, His loved and His own.
Like the stars of the morning, His bright crown adorning,
They shall shine in their beauty, bright gems for His crown.

Your brother in the eternal bonds of Jesus Christ,

Tom Hamblin

CONTENTS

FOREWORD

R ight now you are holding in your hands the thrilling story of an amazing yet ordinary couple. I pray that as you read these pages you will grow in vision, faith, and action.

I have known Tom and Edna Hamblin for many years and they have been a huge blessing to me and our fellow OM workers. They have been pacesetters, especially in the way they have taken risks to get the Word of God to people in difficult, restricted-access nations.

As you read about Tom's childhood you will realize afresh the importance and power of the gospel. Around the world today there are so many individuals like Tom, but without the opportunity he had to be loved by a true believer and introduced to God's good news. I pray that this book will make a difference in all our lives, spurring us to become more involved in compassionate outreach. Lord, let us not be guilty of taking in challenging stories and information and not doing anything about it!

If you are at all interested in the Muslim people and the nations they come from, this is the book for you. I live in London where we have one million Muslim residents, so it's only common sense that I get to know what they are like and what they believe. No matter where you are, Muslims probably live closer than you think – and many are open to friendship.

Because we don't have more people like Tom and Edna there are hundreds of millions of people who have never heard the gospel even once. I pray this book will move many to get more involved in God's great global programme. Where are those who will step into the shoes of Edna and Tom?

It is also my heart's prayer that people who love Jesus and want to see His Word spread will get extra copies of this story to give to others. These days it's not common for young people to buy a book in hard format, but if we share our enthusiasm they might download it onto their phones, PCs or other devices. Gifting them with a hard copy might even encourage them to read a book like this for the first time ever. Others might just happen to see the cover and decide to go online and get a copy. One way or another, we need more people like Tom and Edna who will mobilize people into action. I hope you will be among them.

Dr George Verwer
Founder, Operation Mobilisation (OM International)

INTRODUCTION

As the words of an old hymn declare, "Every virtue we possess and every victory won, and every thought of holiness are His alone."

Paul explained it this way: "I also labour, striving according to his workings, which worketh in me mightily" (Colossians 1:29 KJV). He also wrote that we are workers together with God (see 2 Corinthians 6:1). When he and Barnabas returned to the churches in Antioch and Jerusalem after their first missionary journeys, they reported on "everything that God had done through them" and how He had opened the door of faith to the Gentiles (Acts 14:27; 15:4). They were giving God the praise and also rejoicing that He had worked through them.

On some visits to Arab lands I had the warm companionship of New Zealander David Mitchell, and often felt that we were walking together in the footsteps of Paul and Barnabas. Paul, though, went alone into Arabia for three years and we know nothing of what he did while there. I also made many trips alone throughout the Arabian Gulf during my sixteen years in the region. Three visits were in Saudi Arabia and others took me to Lebanon, Syria, Jordan, Sudan, Oman, and Yemen as well as the United Arab Emirates.

My wife Edna was able to accompany me on a few occasions and in this book you will read about – and laugh over! – one incredible experience we had together at airport customs. My Edna gave her all in Aden, Yemen, when we took on the task of restoring an ancient church and re-establishing Christian worship in that city. We also shared a vision for creating two clinics on the grounds, later completed by others. This ministry has been greatly appreciated and protected by the governing authorities. Verses 10 to 31 of Proverbs chapter 31 sum her up – especially verse 29: "Many women do noble things, but you surpass them all."

If I had time and space I could mention a host of people who received us, sheltered us, stood solidly with us, supported us financially, prayed with us, and took risks on our behalf. They know who they are and do not expect their names to be printed. One particular American I feel I must mention here had a business in Saudi and got me my first visa to enter the country. Within his home, inside a broom and bucket cupboard, there was a secret hatch in the floor that led to an amazing supply of Bibles, New Testaments, and other books and media. He had already been sowing the Word of God for several years and regularly replenishing his supplies. That thrilled me and reminded me that our Abba Father had others in the land who were faithfully scattering His living Word to sustain many precious "diamonds" in the darkness.

I would like to give special thanks to Deborah Meroff. Without her this book would not have been written.

My prayer is that as you read about the actual events in my life and ministry, you will not only be encouraged and blessed but challenged to become actively involved with other missionaries and their endeavours. Though they are all ordinary people, they are doing extraordinary things by the help of the Holy Spirit. In the words of the psalmist: "The Lord has done this, and it is marvellous in our eyes" (Psalm 118:23). To Him be all praise!

I hope you will also discover that it is possible for God to use you to reach out to Muslim men, women, and children where you live. Some of them have been waiting a long time for the truth that can set them free. The appendix at the back of this book is meant to speed you on your way!

Tom Hamblin

1
WELCOME TO ARABIA

E dna and I stood side by side at the Cyprus airport check-in counter, praying silently as I faced the first hurdle of our "mission impossible". Unless we were both one hundred per cent certain that God had commissioned us to courier His life-giving Word to the world's most resistant Arab countries, this would be a fool's errand.

It didn't look good. The luggage of the man in front of me was only 10 kilos overweight and he was forced to pay US$50 in excess charges. When I hefted my 100 kilo-plus boxes onto the scale the airline representative frowned.

"You are very much overweight," she informed me severely.

"Yes. The boxes all contain Bibles and New Testaments."

Unimpressed, the woman stated that I would have to pay an extra $3,000.

"Are you a Christian?" I asked her.

"Yes, I'm a Christian. I'm Greek Orthodox."

"Well, then, you ought to be helping me get these Bibles to where they're needed."

She came down in price to $2,000, but I said I didn't even have that. She consulted with her senior at the next desk.

"You must either pay $1,000 or leave the boxes behind,"

came the ultimatum. There was a whole long queue behind us and everyone was getting embarrassed.

I asked to see their supervisor, hoping he might be another Greek Orthodox Cypriot who would be sympathetic to my plight. Instead, an Arab Muslim in a flowing white robe appeared in front of me. My heart sank.

"What is the matter?" he demanded.

I explained that I was carrying the holy books of God – the Torah [five Books of Moses in the Old Testament], Zabur [Book of Psalms] and Injil [New Testament or Gospels of Jesus] – and I didn't have $1,000 to pay for the extra weight. For a moment the man looked as though he had been struck dumb. Then he turned and gave a dismissive wave to the women at the desks.

"Oh, let him take the books on the aircraft! He will only have to bring them back!"

Edna and I exchanged gleeful smiles and hastened to the departure gate. No charge at all for the excess baggage! I kissed Edna goodbye and boarded the plane.

"Lord," I prayed as I sank into my seat, "you've done the first miracle. Now it's your responsibility to get me through on the other end!"

As the plane lifted off and turned south, towards the desert of the Arabian Peninsula, I had plenty of time to reflect on the mission that God had assigned us in such an extraordinary way.

My wife and I had just finished ten demanding but exhilarating years serving the tribal church in Borneo, known as the "*Sidang Injil Borneo*". I had spent two to three months on that island each year, besides spreading the word among Christian congregations in the United Kingdom, Singapore, and Malaysia. We wanted Christians to understand that the same Holy Spirit who was moving so remarkably in Borneo could also bring times of refreshing where they lived.

Earlier missionaries to that area of Southeast Asia had been the privileged eyewitnesses to transforming revivals, with thousands of indigenous people coming under conviction of their sins and being swept into the kingdom of light. Following up this great work of God, our responsibilities had included raising funds to build jungle Bible schools and provide boats with outboard motors. The boats equipped pastor-evangelists to take the gospel further into the interiors. We also helped wherever needed with medical supplies.

After several years we based ourselves in Singapore and took medical and dental teams to the island for short-term ministry. Volunteers returned home exhausted from working long hours every day, but exhilarated to have seen first-hand the Holy Spirit's power, and its effect on tribal people.

This ministry was not without its humorous moments. I recall a team of eight young and gifted Chinese medical men who joined me early one morning to wash in a local river. We were standing ankle deep in the mud, splashing each other, when a group of children suddenly appeared on the bank and called out to me, using my tribal name, "*Nganid Bala*", which means "The Sharer of Life".

"You should not wash in this part of the river!" they shouted.

"Why not?"

"Because under the mud there are two crocodiles sleeping."

When the Chinese men heard that, they almost jumped out of their skins. They hopped onto the bank in a flash, while I waded ashore. We all had a good laugh and so did the children.

Although the Lord had impressed on Edna and me that we were to serve the tribal church in Borneo for a decade only, He had not revealed what He had in mind after that. When we met for the last time with our Chinese fellowship group in Singapore, we received the first surprising intimation.

We had just begun the prayer meeting in the beautiful home of friends when another participant arrived, bringing a South African Christian whom he'd met earlier in a restaurant and invited along. Near the close of our time together the leader asked Edna and me to kneel in the centre of the room so that everyone could commit us to God and whatever ministry lay ahead.

Suddenly the African stranger spoke up, saying he believed he should pray for us. Everyone was surprised, since no one knew him except the one Chinese brother. But as he interceded his words seemed to contain a prophetic message:

You will now walk in lands that you have never walked before; you will take to the people my Word in their languages. You will experience opposition and threats. You will stand before government rulers and royal princes, and speak of me and declare my Word.

Edna and I, very much struck by this unanticipated message, wrote it down to bring before the Lord. Whenever we received a prophecy like this we tested it by waiting on God and praying that if these words were truly from the Holy Spirit, that He would confirm them. Back in England we also shared the message with friends who joined us in asking where these "lands we had never walked before" might be.

We were open to God's leading. Both of our children, Mark and Sharon, were by now out of the nest and launched in their own careers. After one particular prayer period of three days, as Edna and I separately sought guidance, we were both given the same portion of Scripture from Isaiah chapter 45, the first three verses:

This is what the Lord says to his anointed, to Cyrus, whose right hand I take hold of to subdue nations before him and to strip kings of their armour, to open doors before him so that gates will not be shut: I will go before you and will level the mountains; I will break down gates of bronze and cut through bars of iron. I will give you treasures of darkness, riches stored in secret places, so that you may know that I am the Lord, the God of Israel, who summons you by name.

The phrases that most came alive to us were "open doors", "gates will not be shut", and especially, "I will give you the treasures of darkness, riches stored in secret places." We wondered whether the unknown lands might be China in the Far East, or perhaps Pakistan in South Asia, or another distant and unreached region.

Three weeks later I visited Northern Ireland and was asked to speak on Sunday morning at a small mission hall. Only about a dozen people were there, but as I started the service, in walked two strangers. The regulars must have been thrilled. At the close of my talk one of the visitors stood up and asked to say a few words. He told the group that three years before he had been on his way to commit suicide when he met a man who had given him a tape and said he needed to listen to it.

"I took the tape and I did listen to it. It was your testimony," he said, turning to me. "After that I said to God, if you can work that way in that man's life you can work in mine." Then to my total astonishment he added these words: "The Lord told me those three years ago that when I met you, I must give you a message. I heard you were going to be here today so I came across three counties to be here this morning. This is God's message:

I will take you to lands that you have never walked before, you will take to the people my Word in their languages. You will experience opposition and threats. You will stand before government rulers and royal princes, and speak of me and declare my Word.

I was shaken. This was the identical prophecy that we had heard in Singapore, seven thousand miles away! How could we entertain any doubt that this message was from God?

A little while later a letter came from Lebanon, via Cyprus, inviting Edna and me to share in the ministry of Bible distribution, under the auspices of the Bible Society of Lebanon. We would be based in Cyprus where the Society had a large Bible storage facility and office. But the brief was very explicit. We were "to take the Holy Scriptures in Arabic and other languages and distribute them in the Arabian Gulf" – a place we had never been, just as the prophetic word to us had indicated. With the blessing of our home church in Reading, we moved to Cyprus and prepared to take up the challenge.

* * *

Now I was about to land in one of the most difficult places in the world to take the Word of Life. Inside the terminal I sailed through the airport's immigration check without any problem. On the way to the luggage belts I grabbed a couple of trolleys. Then my boxes started to come through, each one pasted with bright stickers in Arabic that directed, "IMMEDIATE SEARCH". This caught the attention of an Englishman waiting beside me.

"Hey, mate," he said in a broad Yorkshire accent, "why do those boxes have to be opened and searched? What have you got in them?"

"Holy Bibles," I replied, without elaboration. My fellow passenger was clearly shocked.

"Bibles! Blimey! That's worse than whisky! All due respect to you, mate, but don't walk anywhere near me when you go through customs."

When his case appeared on the belt he grabbed it and ran.

At the customs desk, two officers stopped me and my trolleys and wanted to know what I had in the boxes. They demanded that I open each of them. I opened the first box, picked up a copy of the Arabic Bible, and lifted it reverently to my lips.

"The holy Torah, Zabur, and Injil," I told them.

Their eyes widened in astonishment, and the face of one man mottled an ugly red.

"We have no churches here!" he snarled. "We have no Christians here. You are in serious trouble!"

By this time our exchange was attracting considerable interest from other passengers.

"You do not have any churches here," I agreed pleasantly,

"but you do have many Christians. I have come with their holy books."

The officer's voice rose several decibels as he threatened that he was going to see the director of the airport and call the police. He stormed off, leaving his fellow officer leafing through the Bible he had taken from me and reading a portion from the New Testament.

"It's in Arabic!" he marvelled. "Isa [Jesus] is speaking here. Is this the true Injil?" he wanted to know.

When I confirmed that it was, he enquired where I was staying in the city. I knew instantly that this man wanted a copy of the Bible, but he dared not take it in such a public place. I gave him the name of the hotel where I would be lodging for just one night before moving to another address.

"Go – quickly! Go through," he directed. I shot through the customs area without looking back, pushing and pulling my two heavily laden trolleys. The contact people that had been arranged beforehand met me outside and escorted me to my accommodation.

That night the customs officer came to the hotel and asked to see me. He got his Injil – and so did many others in that city.

During the next two weeks I walked through the streets carrying two transparent carrier bags filled with Bibles, so they could be clearly seen. It was the same strategy that I was to employ for the next fifteen years. I put them on tables when I sat. In taxis I sat with a Bible in my hand, reading it. I also entered four- or five-star hotels which always have ground floor hotel coffee shops. Local men can always be found in such places, relaxing and drinking coffee with their friends, sometimes all day. The wives are usually working! I deliberately slowed my steps as I passed tables where they were seated, and someone would invariably call out.

"Are you American?"

"*Salaam Alaikum* [peace be with you], gentlemen! I am British," I would respond, and invariably they would ask me to join them. Arabs are very hospitable.

"Why are you here?" they would then ask as I drank coffee with them. "Who do you work for?"

"I work for a king."

"But you are British; Queen Elizabeth is your royal leader."

"King Isa is the king of all kings and queens throughout the earth," I would smile, explaining that I had come to bring copies of His holy Word to the people here.

I don't really like Arab coffee, but I don't think I ever paid for a cup during all of the years that I followed this routine. In one country a man pulled me aside and said he had to speak with me privately, so we went into the gent's toilet. He looked at me, his eyes filled with tears.

"I have waited for years and years to get a copy of the Injil." He pulled out a roll of money "Here is a thousand dollars. Take this."

I shook my head. "No. You have waited all this time to receive this precious Book, my friend. I can't take one dollar. It is a gift from God."

As I was to learn while serving in His Majesty's Secret Service, God is constantly at work, drawing people to Himself in an amazing variety of ways. A number of Arabs have listened to Christian Bible broadcasts for years, longing to get a copy of the precious Book for themselves. There are no Christian bookshops, so how do they get them?

Some readers may have heard of London City Mission's Tell-a-Tourist ministry. Each year volunteers successfully share the good news of Christ to thousands of visitors to the city through literature distribution, open air preaching, sketchboard talks, and personal evangelism. One of the favourite places to encounter tourists is St James' Park.

On a particular occasion two volunteers sat down next to a Muslim on a park bench and asked if they could share something about Jesus. The Arab listened attentively, accepted a Gospel, and left the UK shortly afterwards for his home country. Later we learned that while he was on the plane the Muslim man read the little Book he had been given. His emotion must have been evident because a cabin attendant stopped to ask if he was all right.

"Yes!" he assured her, beaming through his tears. "I'm seeing things for the first time."

The man read the Gospel through twice during the flight, eager to absorb God's plan of salvation. As soon as he reached home he wrote to the Tell-a-Tourist address written in the Gospel's flyleaf, asking for the name of someone he could talk with.

Shortly after that Edna and I were surprised to get a letter from the London ministry. We didn't know anyone with Tell-a-Tourist and had no idea how they had got our names. But since I was given the telephone number of the Arab interested in a contact, I decided to call him on my next trip.

"We have some mutual friends in London," I told the man on the phone, after a brief introduction.

"Oh!" came the excited response. *"You must be my brother in Christ! You must come to my office!"*

I tracked down the address in the city and went inside. A

number of Arab men were in the lobby but my newfound friend spotted me and cried out at once, "You must be my brother Tom!"

He conducted me to an opulent office. Once we were alone I took out the full Arabic Bible that I had brought with me, and with tears he took it in his hands. Then he got down on his knees on the carpet and thanked God.

"Show me where we will start our first study of the Bible!" he urged me, as he rose.

I opened to the fifth chapter of Romans:

> Therefore, since we have been justified through faith, we have peace with God through our Lord Jesus Christ through whom we have gained access by faith into this grace in which we now stand (verses 1–2).

The man marvelled; it was all such a revelation to him. Eventually we reached chapter eight:

> Therefore, there is now no condemnation for those who are in Christ Jesus, because through Christ Jesus the law of the Spirit who gives life has set you free from the law of sin and death. For what the law was powerless to do because it was weakened by the flesh, God did by sending his own Son in the likeness of sinful flesh to be a sin offering (verses 1–3).

My new friend fell once more to his knees. "You are my Abba Father!" he cried worshipfully, pouring out his thanks and joy to the Lord for setting his spirit free. He begged me to bring another copy of the Bible for a senior minister he knew. Since I had a few extra copies with me I handed them over. Later, Alexander – the Christian name this man decided to take in addition to his Arabic names – did indeed give a Bible to the minister, who said he'd like to meet me.

I had wonderful fellowship with Alexander and he wrote to me several times. In his last letter he said, "I must do what I can for you now, because I know my time is short." Then I heard no more. When I tried to find him on my next visit to his country I was simply told that he and his family were "gone". I have not seen or heard from him since.

Looking back at all the years that I served as God's courier to the Muslim world, I can affirm that I never had to pay a single dollar of overweight charges to an airline for carrying a shipment of Bibles. The various airline staff at the international airport in Larnaca, Cyprus, got to know me as "the Bible man". Nor was a single copy of God's Word permanently confiscated at the other end. The Lord faithfully fulfilled His part of the bargain, smoothing the way before us in lands we had never walked before.

2

A ROUGH START IN READING

In the same historic year of 1936 that the King of England abdicated his throne, a woman gave birth to her fifth son on the attic mattress of a run-down house in Reading. I was an unwanted child, another mouth to feed in our hungry household. My father already had a family when he seduced my mother, so I and my three older brothers (the first boy having died at eleven months) all bore the stamp of illegitimacy. The boys at school made sure I didn't forget it. I remember going to my mother to ask why they called her a prostitute. For some reason my birth wasn't even registered until I was twelve.

Our father was a property auctioneer but most of his pay went on drink, so we experienced tough times as we grew up. He often got us kids up at dawn to pick mushrooms in the fields nearby. After we filled the baskets he went off to sell them at the market and bought alcohol while we ran off to school, eating raw mushrooms for breakfast.

I remember my brothers and I hiring a large wheelbarrow for six or nine pennies a day during school holidays, and pushing it out to where the "posh folks" lived. Their spacious homes and beautifully landscaped gardens were only a mile or two away but a world apart from the damp and crowded quarters we rented, with its brick backyard. Putting on our best behaviour, we went door to door and politely asked residents if they had any old rags, clothes, rabbit skins, metal items or jam jars they wanted to dispose of.

Sometimes we were asked who we were collecting for, so my older brothers always told them it was for the boys' brigade or the scouts. Of course the truth was that we were the primary beneficiaries. After we trundled our wheelbarrow home Mother would carefully go through the contents, giving a glad exclamation whenever she found clothing that she could repair for us to wear, especially through the winter months. She also occasionally found some ladies' underclothing or a dress that she could alter and wear herself. In all the years I knew her as a child and youth she never had anything new, and neither did we. Most of the rest of our haul we took to a scrap yard. The owners paid us a penny for four jam jars and three to six pennies for rabbit skins, depending on their quality. We also earned a little for rags and bits of metal; a little more for old woollen clothing.

For six Christmases we didn't bother to hang up stockings; there were no apples or oranges to look forward to. My seventh year was a little better because my father got some money from stolen goods. Mum supplemented the family income by doing the neighbours' washing for six pennies a load. Everything had to be washed by hand over a tub – backbreaking work. She didn't do much ironing as it took a long time to heat the old-fashioned irons on a hot stove. Usually she managed two or three loads a day.

Life was not easy for our mother. Sometimes Dad would come home drunk and demand money from her. She would tell him that she hadn't taken in any washing that day and he would turn to us to verify if this was true. Of course we always backed up our mum, knowing she had hidden her sixpenny coins somewhere out of sight. Dad would then hit her hard, calling her a liar and other terrible names. Whenever he was drunk on beer he turned belligerent and nasty, sometimes picking up the dinner she had carefully prepared and kept warm on the stove and flinging it all over the wall. But if he had gotten drunk on spirits he was brutal.

My eldest brother Brian was my hero, for he would defend Mum as much as he could and shield her from blows by taking them himself. Often he went to school with a split lip, bruised face or black eye, and although his teachers might be sympathetic they never intervened with what went on at home. Today my father would have been hauled off to the police station and Brian sent to a hospital.

My next-oldest brother, Ron, also got some beatings, but Ray, my third brother, never got the belt. For some reason he seemed to be Dad's favourite. He just walked away whenever things got bad for our mother. As for myself, the time came when I too learned to stand up to my dad, even when I contracted TB at the age of nine and was in and out of hospital for two years, attending an open-air school. Later I repented of what I did to him. Although God forgave me my father did not until years later, when he himself was born anew.

All through our childhood and into our teens we made do with second-hand clothes and shoes. Underwear was a luxury we dispensed with unless Mum happened to find some among the rags we gathered. Our old shoes, however, posed the biggest problem. Whenever they got holes in them Mum could not afford to take them to a cobbler, so every day she collected cardboard boxes from the shops and cut out soles to place in the bottom of our shoes. She also gave us a spare pair to hide in the tops of our trousers, which were held up with string. When it rained and our feet got wet we replaced the cardboard soles with the spares. Of course if other children saw us doing this they mocked us, so we had a few fights.

Our main diet consisted of potatoes, cabbages, carrots, tripe, and pigs' trotters and intestines (called chittlings). Once a week we got horse meat and often ate rabbits and the scrag end of mutton. Dad alone got better meat, and woe betide everyone if he didn't! We also ate a lot of bread with dripping. Mum would get animal fat from the butcher and render it in a pan over the fire, pouring off the fat into bowls. When it had set solid, we scraped it onto slices of bread. To this day I still love bread and dripping, with a sprinkle of salt and mustard! In addition, each night before going to bed we ate a raw onion. Mum also sliced an onion to put on a saucer in our bedroom, for it was a popular belief that onions would attract all the germs to themselves, thus creating a healthier space.

She tried her best. Every Saturday night she insisted on bringing in the tin bath from the back yard. This was filled with water she boiled on our old brick copper, and my three brothers all went in before me. As you might imagine, the water was less than hot or clean by the time it was my turn to climb in!

For some years the four of us boys slept on a mattress on the attic floor, all laying top to toe in opposite directions. We had fun tickling toes and feet, and the togetherness we shared resulted in close bonding.

One morning as we were eating our bread and jam or

cereal before going to school, Brian came down the old staircase looking as white as a ghost and told Mum he felt ill. He seemed to be staggering, and could eat nothing. Dad clipped him round the ear and told him in foul language to get off to school, there was nothing wrong with him but laziness.

In actual fact, the rest of us weren't so well, either. We all had sore throats and runny noses. As usual, we used rags as handkerchiefs and threw them away when they were no further use. Mum whispered to our oldest brother to go on up the road as if he were going to school, then cut across to the road that led to the school clinic. Brian followed her instructions and approached the nurse at reception. The clinic was full of mothers with children, but the nurse took one look and immediately ran to get a doctor, who lost no time calling an ambulance. Brian was dangerously ill with diphtheria. The clinic had to be closed for two weeks and fumigated, and everyone who was there that day was given an inoculation. The incident got quite a write-up in the local papers.

Meanwhile, more ambulances with nurses came looking for the rest of us, and we three boys were also diagnosed with diphtheria. Dad and Mum hadn't contracted the disease, but the medics found Mum in urgent need of having her gall bladder removed. Although she was ill she always hid her troubles from us as much as possible. We brothers were taken to an isolation hospital. We had a ward to ourselves but they separated us, one in each corner. Then they strapped us in bed after laying us on our right sides to avoid strain on our hearts, and hand-fed us. They also gave us injections and enemas, morning and evening, which we didn't care for at all. Even parents were not allowed in to visit, they could only look at us through closed windows. Our dad came to see us only once in thirty days and since Mum was in another hospital for five weeks, she was unable to visit. Three of us were sent home after four weeks and it was difficult to cope, not having her there. Poor as our circumstances were, our mother was the love and light of our world. Brian, who was apparently the carrier of the disease, was the last of us pronounced fit enough to return home. We all thought he was going to die. I cried a lot for I loved him very much. What an explosion of joy I experienced when he finally walked through the back door! I hugged him and did not want to let go.

"I am okay now, Tommy," he reassured me. "All we need now is for Mum to come home from the hospital too." It seemed ages before she did, and I tortured myself with fears that she had gone away for good.

Later, when they were teenagers, Brian and Ron both ran away from home. Eventually one went into the merchant navy and the other joined the army. They returned to visit only for Mum's sake, and hid money around the old, damp house where only she could find it. She shed many tears each time they left again. I would put my arms around her and cry with her.

My brother Ray was also looking forward to escaping to two years of national service when he turned eighteen. Whenever Dad was aggressive and abusive he simply walked away and lost himself somewhere with friends. It was left to me to protect Mum as much as I could.

But God in His mercy found a way to reach into my life. During my early teens I worked part time selling newspapers on street corners in the centre of Reading, and there was always some religious group singing or speaking from a soapbox on one of the other corners. After the meeting one particular man would come over to speak to me and I'd pretend I hadn't heard a word they'd said. But I was lying, for I had listened. What's more I had liked what I'd heard. Harry Harrison invited me to his home on Sunday afternoons, along with other teenage boys and sometimes girls. He and his wife had no children of their own.

I shall never forget my first visit. As we gathered at a table spread with sandwiches and desserts, our host – whom we called Holy Harry – bowed his head and prayed. We looked at each other and I immediately heard a voice inside me say, "This man knows God." I marvelled at that inner witness, and eventually the truth of those words was confirmed again and again. Harry never preached at us, but we saw the truth of the gospel by the way he lived.

At sixteen I was the last son left at home. Ray had joined the army and I had been working since leaving school at fifteen, lifting boxes in a food warehouse and still selling papers part time. I was determined to earn enough to help my mother, whom I loved with my whole heart. By this time though I was also interested in learning about Jesus Christ and what He had done for the world – myself included. A group of us that Harry had befriended had started going along to his church. The first message I heard was from 2 Corinthians 5:17: "Therefore, if anyone is in Christ, he is a new creation: The old has gone, the new has come!"

One night when I returned from a youth Bible study I found my father attacking my mother. It looked like he was half killing her. I immediately grabbed a large poker and jumped between them, forcing my dad to the ground and beating him.

"You'll kill him, Tom. Stop it!" my mother screamed, putting her arms around my waist and holding me as she cried and pleaded with me. I was like a raging bull as years of deep hatred took over.

Our next-door neighbours came through the door. It was like that in those days; we were always in and out of each other's homes. When there were domestic flare-ups they usually kept clear. But not this time. The police were called from a phone booth round the corner, since no one in our neighbourhood had private phones. They arrived in a car with an ambulance following, and Dad was taken to hospital. I was put in a police car and as we drove off, the big sergeant sitting in front turned in his seat.

"Where do your grandparents live, lad ? Or your uncles and aunties?"

"I ain't got any. Never had any because I'm a bastard," I flung the words defiantly.

"Now listen, son," said the sergeant, "I'm trying to help you. Who is your best friend?"

Immediately I thought of Harry Harrison and his wife, who had invited me and other fellows to his home for afternoon tea, and ran a young people's meeting in the local Baptist church. The policeman insisted that I tell him where they lived. I tried to refuse but he won out and ordered the driver to take me to Mr Harrison's address. I was beginning to think the policeman knew him, and wondered if maybe Holy Harry had been in trouble with the police himself!

When we arrived at the Harrisons' it was past midnight and all the houses on the street were in darkness. In those days most people stayed at home in the evenings, not like today where so many are still out on the streets, in pubs and eating places that are open most of the night. The sergeant towed me to the front door and started knocking loudly. A light went on upstairs, then downstairs. The door opened abruptly and there was Holy Harry, looking at us in shock. Small wonder – my shirt was covered in blood and I was still trembling with anger.

"Mr Harrison," stated the sergeant, "I understand you know this young man and you've been a friend to him. Now, I could take him away for three days, until it's time for him to appear in juvenile court, but would you be willing to take responsibility for him?" I was looking at Mr Harrison and wondering why he was wearing a coat. It was actually a dressing gown, but I had never seen one before. That dressing gown is still in my possession, and I continue to show it in meetings when I am giving my testimony.

Uncle Harry simply opened his arms wide and said, "Tom, my dear boy – come in." As I began to step towards him he threw his arms around me and gave me a strong embrace. It was the first time anyone had ever hugged me. My father had never shown affection to any of us, and our mother was always too busy – and too tired – trying to feed and care for us. The embrace electrified me. I knew this was compassion and genuine welcome.

Harry's wife, Grace, called from the upstairs bedroom, "Who is it, Harry?"

When he replied, "It's Tom, dear," she came running down the stairs. I remember her hair was in metal curlers, which I had never seen before. My mother always used rag curlers. She hastily drew some warm water into a bowl and with Harry's help took off my shirt to gently bathe my wounds as I wept.

"Tom," said Harry. "You know what is the answer for your father?"

"Yes!" I replied. "Get a double decker bus to run over him and finish him off!"

"No, Tom. You both need to know Jesus as your Saviour, let Him save you from your sins and make you a new person, with new desires and delights."

I was not convinced then, but a day came not long afterward when I was home alone that I knelt by an old chair and with tears cried out – first to God, then to Jesus, asking Him to clean me up, come into me, and make me the man I ought to be. He did come and fill my heart and I knew something wonderful had happened.

Holy Harry visited my father in hospital and told him firmly that he had brought his injuries upon himself through his years of cruelty to his family. Dad dropped the charges against me, so there was no court case. What a good thing he did, for I had been to juvenile court before, caught for stealing some items from a house with another boy. I was warned on that occasion that if I appeared in court again I would be sent to a special school.

It was the beginning of a new dawn. My father never again laid a hand on my mother, even when I was away for two years of military service in the Far East. Mum wrote a letter to me each week during that period. I still have those letters, and when occasionally I open the box and read a couple of them, emotion overcomes me. I weep, and cannot read further.

Meanwhile, during those transitional years between

youth and manhood, Mr Harrison became my spiritual
father. He gave me unconditional love, discipled me, and
taught me how to pray. He shared the words of the old hymn
by George Matheson, "Make me your captive, Lord, and
then I shall be free; force me to render up my sword and
I shall conqueror be. I sink in life's alarms when by myself
I stand, imprison me within Thine arms and strong shall
be my hand." He explained that only when I was willing to
surrender my will to God's and become His captive, could
I experience total freedom to walk as His child. One day,
he told me, my hatred for my father would turn to pity and
compassion, and I would love him and pray for his salvation.
And that is exactly what happened.

Almost eight years later Dad and Mum came and stayed
with us for a week in Bournemouth, where Edna and I were
working in a Christian guest house. On Sunday I asked him
to go with me to an evening service in a well-known Baptist
church, where the pastor was a man of God who preached
very effectively with down-to-earth language. Mum and
Edna also urged him to go with me. He agreed and though
we got there almost thirty minutes before the service began,
it was filling up. We were given two seats in the third row
from the front.

When Pastor Dixon began to speak he gave a gripping
introduction to his sermon. "I have a message for a man
here tonight, or many men, but perhaps one in particular."
I wanted to stand up and shout, "You are so right! He's
sitting here beside me, my father!" The Holy Spirit welled
up within me, confirming to me that this was the night of
Dad's salvation... and it was! Hallelujah.

We walked home that evening arm in arm, something

that had never happened before. He kept stopping under the street lights, confessing his sins all over again, his wickedness to Mum and his sons. I showed him Scriptures that reassured him, such as "I [the Lord] will repay you for the years the locusts have eaten", and "the blood of Jesus, his Son, cleanses us from all sin."[1]

There was redemption, reconciliation, and re-creation before God that night. I told my dad that I had forgiven him, as God had, and when we got to the guest house he went through the door and looked at my mother and said, "Alice, can you forgive me too?"

She embraced him and gently stroked his face. "George, we'll start over again."

Mum had cancer, and only had a short while left on earth. But she passed into the presence of her Saviour with peace and enjoyed her remaining time with a transformed husband, who joined her in heaven two years later. We wait with anticipation to be reunited one day in glory. How great is the wonderful grace of our God!

---

1 Joel 2:25; 1 John 1:7

3
COMMISSIONED AND RE-COMMISSIONED

I had first gotten to know Edna Streams at Coley School in Reading, when I was about twelve. I sat in a desk right behind her. She was not favourably impressed by me and no wonder. I was a real nuisance to her and the girl she sat with. When Edna was fifteen she told all her friends to have nothing to do with Tommy Hamblin – he was the most horrible boy at school. She was telling the truth.

A lot can happen in three years. By the time we were both eighteen Edna and I had both allowed Jesus Christ to turn our lives around – and we were very much in love with each other. Such is the grace of God! I had only ten pounds to spend on an engagement ring but Edna was unfazed. The ring she chose cost nine pounds and we used the remaining money to celebrate in a restaurant with egg on toast and cups of tea.

We had great plans, of course, even though Edna's mother was totally shocked that her daughter had fallen in love with one of the notorious Hamblin boys. Edna's father wouldn't allow us to marry until I did my stint in the army. In those days every man in the United Kingdom was expected to enlist for National Service. In January 1955, at the age of eighteen, it was my turn.

Besides the usual childhood diseases my health history

included pneumonia, rheumatic fever, diphtheria, and TB, from which I was not declared fully fit until I was seventeen. Seven doctors examined me and they all had different opinions about my eligibility for the service, a few stating I had a heart murmur. Finally I was sent to see a top specialist from London. When I met him I knew he had been drinking and it wasn't lemonade: he had the tell-tale signs of a blue, bulbous nose and slurred speech. He also smelt like a brewery.

"Well, young man," the doctor observed after examining me, "you are either going to be a good athlete or you'll die suddenly."

To my surprised gratification he signed me off for the army as A1 – fit as a fiddle.

I received basic training in the Royal Army Medical Corps at Crookham Camp in Hampshire. Deciding to take a stand for my faith right from the start, I knelt down beside my bed, with my Bible, and prayed. When I opened my eyes there was another fellow kneeling on the other side of the bed. Together we worked on the rest of the men, and others joined us each night around my bunk.

My first duty as a new recruit was cleaning toilets and urinals. There was no end to these and they were all smelly. The first time I went about this assignment I was on my own, so I sang to keep myself motivated. I was on my hands and knees and midway through singing "Shining for Jesus, shining all the time" when I suddenly heard a gruff command behind me.

"Soldier, come here!"

I straightened to attention and found my staff sergeant staring at me oddly. He told me to relax and to sit down on the sink. I felt quite nervous but obeyed.

"Tell me, private," he asked. "How can you sing about 'Jesus' and 'shining' when you're doing the filthiest job there is?"

So I told him, as simply as I could, how my life had turned around when I gave it to Jesus at the age of sixteen and a half. Sergeant Smalley listened intently, then nodded.

"I'm married to a French Catholic lady," he said thoughtfully. "She's religious too. But I'd like to know more about why Jesus can make such a difference in a man. Come and see me in my office when you're done here, after lunch, and tell your sergeant that I need you this afternoon for more duties."

As soon as I reported back from my assignment that day, however, I was ordered to pick up my kit bag and travel up to Liverpool. There I was to board the HMV *Devonshire* and sail for Singapore. I implored my sergeant to let me go back to see Staff Smalley. He refused, swore at me, and said if I didn't hurry I would miss the military train to Liverpool. I was deeply disappointed, knowing I would probably never meet Sergeant Smalley again.

I got on that crowded troop ship knowing only one other soldier. John Taylor was also a Christian and he would one day become a missionary to the Lap people in the northern parts of Norway, Sweden, and Russia. When we discovered there was no chaplain on board, I decided to write a letter to the captain to ask if I could conduct services. My schooling hadn't been the best. I could not spell "interdenominational" and for that matter didn't understand what it meant. However, John made the necessary corrections and I put the letter into the ship's internal mailbox.

Before long I heard an announcement blaring over the

communication system: "Would Private T. Hamblin report to the adjutant's office, immediately!"

I reported, and was informed I'd been ordered to see the "Old Man" – the captain.

"Stand at ease, Hamblin," this superior told me after I entered his office with some trepidation, accompanied by the adjutant.

"So, you'd like to conduct services on board." He looked me over. "Did you not know that when there's no chaplain, the captain takes the services?"

"No, sir. I did not. Do you preach the gospel, sir?"

"No," he hesitated slightly in answering. "We have prayers and a couple of hymns and read a psalm. What would you like to do?"

"Have you heard of Billy Graham, Captain?" I queried, and he nodded.

"That's what I'd like to do. Give a message with the gospel in an understandable way, like Billy Graham does."

"Have you been ordained, Hamblin?"

I didn't know what he meant, so I said I hadn't.

Then he asked, "You'd like to sing, too? Because we have plenty of hymn books."

"Yes, sir. My friend has a mouth organ, and I know someone else who has a banjo." He grinned at that but the adjutant only looked rattled.

The captain turned to him. "Tell everyone that Hamblin will hold services on Sunday evening on troop deck. Announce it on the ship's speakers and put it in the daily orders – if that's okay with you, Private Hamblin?"

"Yes, sir!" I replied, a wide smile spreading over my face.

Later the captain called me back and gave me the keys to

the chaplain's office, in case any of the men wanted to talk with me. I was to be in that office each day while we were at sea. We also got the use of the hymn books. John and I felt overwhelmed. We agreed between us that I would give a testimony and he could give a little message.

That first evening only about twenty of us gathered on deck for the service. However, the bridge above us filled up with listening officers and wives.

I knew there were at least six hundred Welshmen on board so we decided to sing the old Welsh favourite, "Guide Me, O Thou Great Jehovah". That hymn was like waving a red rag in front of a bull. Nearly every one of those Welshmen promptly deserted what they were doing and poured onto the deck. Those troops didn't just lift their voices for that hymn; they sang it in glorious, two-part harmony! So we sang some more songs. They couldn't get enough. I followed with my testimony and John gave a simple five or six minute talk. Then we invited the listeners to give their lives to Christ.

The first man to step forward and kneel down was the regiment's champion boxer. Not only did men get saved on that ship, but the chaplain's office was used continuously for counselling. We also had Bible study, prayers, and fellowship every night.

Nineteen months later I was on a beach when someone came to tell me an officer was looking for me, a Captain Halliday. He led the way and when the captain and I were sitting down he said, "I was on the bridge of the *Devonshire*, Hamblin, when you and your friend held your services. I listened to you those four Sundays at sea. I could have talked to you then, but I was an officer and you a private. Afterwards I was posted up in North Malaya but I couldn't forget what you said. There was a Brethren missionary there, from Bournemouth. I went to see him, and he led me to the Lord Jesus."

Don Halliday and I remained friends for years after that encounter. He and his wife became medical missionaries with OMF to North Malaya and Southern Thailand, serving for eleven years, I think. Perhaps more. They were delightful people.

As for Staff Sergeant Joe Smalley, first encountered while I was toilet-cleaning, we met again on my last morning in Singapore before returning to the UK. I had been asked to speak at a Sunday morning service in "Bethesda", a Brethren gospel hall, and when I came out of the building at the end of it I saw a hand stretched out to greet me.

"Staff Smalley!" I exclaimed in surprise.

"Don't call me Staff Smalley," he instructed, smiling. "Call me Brother Joe."

He asked why I hadn't gone back to see him that day, after my cleaning duties, and then he went on to explain how God had brought a born-again corporal into his unit very soon after I sailed.

"He was the one who brought me through to Christ," said Joe Smalley. "Then my wife accepted Him, and all of the rest of my family. I wanted you to know."

I had the joy of leading many to the Lord while I was in the military, even though I was still wet behind the ears. When a new soldier arrived in our barrack room in Singapore, fresh from England, we all welcomed him and briefed him about the work we were engaged in, supplying hospitals and medical field ambulances in the jungles of Malaya. He was a very pleasant young Jewish man, full of questions, and he worked conscientiously. I liked him very much. He sometimes joined me for a swim at the Sandes Soldiers' Christian Centre and we enjoyed the friendship. Nobody got on his back or made detrimental remarks.

One day he asked me why I had so many posters up beside my bed about God and Jesus. He had also noticed the leaflets on my locker with the sign, "Please Take a Tract". I had a few good times of sharing with him why I was so overt about my faith in Jesus, the Son of God, sent by the Father to be the Saviour of the world. We never argued, even once. I got him a Bible and he often read it, sometimes for long periods. I did not interrupt him but inwardly claimed the verse, "The unfolding of your words gives light" (Psalm 119:130).

One evening he came over to my bed in the barrack room, sat down, and said, "Tom, I do believe Jesus is my Messiah." Naturally I was bursting with joy that he had made such a definite, clear confession, for I had not pressured him in any way. The other men in the room were listening to our conversation and looking at us quizzically. No doubt some were thinking, "Oh, no, not another religious loony. It's bad enough having Tom!"

This Jewish soldier who became my brother in Christ was a gentleman; I mean by that he was a real man with a gentle nature. One night a few days later we had a powerful tropical monsoon storm complete with thunder, lightning, and torrential rain. He jumped off his bed, shouting loudly, "Tom, wake up, our Lord Jesus is coming back again!"

I got up and stood beside him and said something like, "If it is tonight we will go together to meet Him in the air."

One or two of the other soldiers mocked, "It's not tonight, so go back to bed!"

We waited together as the storm eventually subsided, then after a prayer we returned to our beds. He was brave and outspoken to the other men, reminding them they came from a Christian background and yet did not believe in Jesus Christ as their Saviour. I sensed they felt sheepish and perhaps ashamed.

Soon after this he had sad news from home – I think a death in the family. He was given compassionate leave but did not return. Sadly, I never heard from him again. But I know for sure my friend had become a messianic believer, with his whole heart.

One Sunday during my time in Singapore we soldiers were all marched to church, regardless of our denominational affiliation. The new chaplain who spoke to us was clearly of a liberal persuasion, for not only was his message devoid of the gospel, but he also used suggestive and offensive innuendo.

At last, unable to restrain myself, I jumped up and rebuked the chaplain. I stated that it was his responsibility as a man of God to share the good news of Christ. Not stopping at that, I accused the man of possessing an unclean mind.

My sergeant friend sitting behind me murmured that I was in for it, and sure enough, the chaplain angrily confronted me.

"How dare you?" he hissed, pointing to the pips on his shoulder.

"Those are given to officers and gentlemen," I returned, "and you are neither."

Afterwards the other soldiers came in a body to support me. "We decided that if we wanted to learn about Jesus," they told me, "we'd come to you. We're all behind you!"

Nevertheless it wasn't long before I was marched to the major's office, quick-time.

"Who do you think you are, ruining a divine act of worship?" he demanded as I stood to attention.

"Sir, there was nothing divine about it," I answered respectfully. "It was from the devil."

The major hit the desk so hard with his cane that it broke. I got seven days confined to barracks and lots of stinking jobs to do. But I kept in good spirits, singing and whistling hymns and choruses.

Later, this same officer called me in and put me in charge of the keys to the dangerous drugs store and the vaccines. He said I was the only man he could trust. But although the responsibility should have made me a sergeant, the major refused to promote me.

"If only you didn't have these outside interests," he complained.

"It's an inside interest, what I've got inside me," I told him. But he wouldn't listen. Only when he moved on did he admit, "I wish you and I could have got on." He was a Roman Catholic and went to mass regularly, so I think he found my extrovert Christianity uncomfortable, as well as my stand against alcohol.

When the major's replacement came, within twenty-four hours he wanted to know why I hadn't been promoted to sergeant for the job I was doing. I said, "Perhaps you should ask Captain Malloy" (the next officer in command).

The colonel shouted to Malloy who simply responded, "They couldn't see eye to eye."

The new colonel offered to promote me immediately if I would sign on for another year of service. But I was due to go home in a month and explained that I was engaged. Edna and I both wanted to serve as missionaries once we were married. I don't regret making that decision, not in a thousand years, though it meant I never rose above the dizzy rank of private. I was not always an obedient soldier, but I believe I was obedient to the Lord Jesus.

I was demobilized in January 1957 and the wedding took place on 8 June, when we were both twenty. I had forked out the money for a wedding suit during the January sales and carefully laid the suit away for the big day. My pastor and his wife kindly gave me the use of their bath on the morning of the wedding, since we didn't have one in my mother's house. What bliss! Then came the moment to put on my bargain suit. I hadn't tried it on since its purchase, and horror of horrors, it no longer fit me around the waist! Over the last six months of eating proper English food instead of army fare, without the diet of powdered milk and rice we were given in the tropics, I had gained weight. What to do? Only an hour remained before the ceremony. Too embarrassed to tell the pastor and best man, I left my top trouser button undone, hidden by my jacket. The jacket was tight across the back, but the wedding photos were all taken from the front so I got away with it – just!

For the next two years I worked with a man named Charlie Potter, a well-known former Communist who had accepted Christ at a 1954 Billy Graham crusade at White City Stadium, London. Shortly after that momentous decision he had walked to the front of my church in Reading and made an open confession. Charlie made up his mind to preach Christ wherever he had previously preached Communism. Edna and I felt God wanted me to minister alongside Charlie and the Worker's Christian Fellowship that he was representing.

Charlie and I travelled all over the UK, speaking in factories, shipyards, and collieries. I well remember the first open-air meeting he instructed me to take, to a big audience of shipyard workers. I protested that I had no training, and that he should do the speaking himself.

"You don't need training; you've got the Holy Spirit!" Charlie shot back. "God says, 'Open your mouth, and I will fill it.' And you should thank God, Tom Hamblin, because you have a big mouth!"

There were two thousand or more men at that meeting. I marvelled to see the tears on many of their faces as I gave them the gospel message. Some shouted out in public for forgiveness. Another man cried, "Keep preaching, Sonny!"

Charlie did a lot to help me make evangelism part of my lifestyle. "You have an inferiority complex," he once told me, "and God does not give inferiority complexes, Tom. You have conviction, so be bold." Charlie was called home to glory suddenly one Saturday afternoon, when he was only forty-eight. My heart was so overwhelmed with sorrow, I wept on and off for many days. I was not too well at this time and the doctor told me if I did not get three months' rest I would be in a wooden box myself.

Our first child, Sharon, was born after two years of marriage. Edna and I had struggled to live on the small salary we earned with Charlie, and now he was gone. I found work with a rodent control company called Rentokil. One time a wealthy man I met on a job offered to sell me a classic Model T Ford for just five pounds. I didn't have five pounds but it was too good a deal to miss so I borrowed the money from my mates. Edna wasn't happy about this transaction and when I brought the car home to where we lived, she wept. We didn't have enough money to run a car, she explained. Making ends meet was tough even without this extra burden.

However, a medical missionary came to our church within a week and shared that he was raising funds to build an extension to a small hospital in Africa. He needed a car to get around the UK. I told him privately that I had a car, and showed it to him. He couldn't believe that I was willing to part with my excellent car for free. He drove it away rejoicing in God's provision.

Of course, I still had to pay back my two mates who had loaned me the five pounds to buy the car. They thought I was crazy to give it away! I think I gave the money back at five shillings a week, split between the two of them. They were good men themselves, however, and admired me as a man of faith.

Many years later I was asked to speak to the Hospital Christian Fellowship at the Royal Berkshire Hospital in Reading. A good number of people attended, and afterwards an older man came to talk to me.

"Do you remember me, Tom?" asked a Dr Peter Williams. "Many years ago you gave me a car."

I then told him how I came to own the car. He was deeply moved.

The doctor's eyes filled with tears as he recounted his story. "We used that car whenever we were in the UK for deputation over the next twenty years, and it never let us down. We built that clinic in Africa, although, sadly, rebels later burned it down."

After our meeting Dr Williams wrote me a beautiful letter and enclosed a cheque for £100 as accrued "interest" on my investment of the car. But you can never out-give God. Some time after giving away that Ford I received a note in the post from an American lady I'd never met, stating that God had told her to give me a car for my open-air ministry. Her cheque was enclosed. She added, "Don't thank me. Get on your knees and thank God."

When we left this ministry I wrote to the donor and offered to give the car back to her, by selling it and sending the proceeds. She responded, "Sell it, and use the money for whatever is next." I could not do that but I knew of a missionary doing open-air rural village evangelism and he desperately needed a vehicle, for his very old one was near useless. So I gave the car to him.

Edna and I spent 1963 in Bournemouth running a Christian guest house for holidays. Our son Mark was born that year. Then, seeing the military as a huge mission field and obeying the Lord's leading, we signed up with Sandes Soldiers' and Airmen's Centres and the four of us moved to Northern Ireland. It was during the next four years that I truly understood the importance of prayer and fasting for effective service to God.

The Sandes outreach to military personnel was born in 1865 through the concern of a young Irish schoolgirl named Elise Sandes, who prayed for soldiers with her parents. Men in the military had an unsavoury reputation among the general populace in those days, but God put it in Elise's heart to invite them to meetings in her own home, with her parents' permission. As she began to understand the needs, temptations, and loneliness that confront young men serving away from home, her conviction grew that God's people needed to win them through the love of Christ.

Despite limited funds and a shortage of helpers, Elise Sandes started opening soldiers' homes from 1869. These were truly a "Home from Home". Her goal was that young men would experience the reality of knowing Jesus through the unconditional loving service provided by Christian volunteers.

From the first home in Tralee, County Kerry, other centres and homes sprang up all over Ireland, then crossed to England. Before long the ministry spread to bases in South Africa, India, Southeast Asia, Jamaica, Iceland, and France. The British military establishment, recognizing the important contribution that Sandes Soldiers' and Airmen's Centres made to the welfare of enlisted men, warmly welcomed their presence.

Edna and I agreed to move overseas to Singapore in 1968. The first Sandes Home, covering seven acres and including a full-sized swimming pool and accommodation for up to eighty, was established in 1949. We opened two smaller Sandes centres in other military camps on the island. As Far East directors we lived in Singapore but I travelled often. One centre that we opened on a Hong Kong island had previously been used for lepers, under the care of The Leprosy Mission, Scotland. When we asked the governor if we could rent one of the islands off shore to use as a Christian centre for military personnel, he agreed to a ten-year lease. Five or six years later, however, authorities reclaimed the island property in order to accommodate an influx of Vietnamese boat people. We also opened homes in Sabah and Sarawak, known also as Borneo.

People of all nationalities often came to visit our centres and find out about our work. Once a group of young Asian lads about eighteen years old walked in. These were "sprogs" – new army recruits, wearing their green uniforms – and they wanted to know if they could come to our Christian centre. Of course we told them they were very welcome; we wanted to serve all the military. Many were introduced to the Lord and chose to follow Him. One lad later became a curate and then a fully ordained priest in the Anglican Church. Others also served as church elders and pastors.

Years later I got a surprise phone call from one of these men; he was visiting the UK and wanted to see me. What a delight to reunite and catch up with each other after so long. When he gave me his card I saw that he was now dean of a cathedral in Singapore. Since then he has become a bishop, a humble man of God with immense love and vision for mission to the unreached in Asia and the Middle East.

I felt our meeting was ordained by God. I told him all about my friend who was a gifted evangelical Anglican priest in Kuwait at the time. I had just received a letter from him the day before to say he was going to Singapore to challenge Christians to minister in the Middle East. So many thousands of mainland Chinese were going to work in the Arab world, and finding Christ there. They needed pastors and literature translated into Mandarin.

The dean nearly leapt out of his seat with excitement when he heard this. The pair of them were able to meet up in Singapore, and God used this contact to fulfil His purposes.

* * *

During our period of service in Singapore we sometimes had to minister in some very delicate family situations. When the wife of one very happily married couple in the military had a nervous breakdown, the medical officer decided she would have to be sent back to the UK. Her husband loved her dearly but did not want to leave the island. A neighbour friend of theirs who was a keen Christian and regularly attended services at our Christian centre urged him, "You should go over to the Sandes Soldiers' and Airmen's Home and ask Tom and Edna Hamblin to pray for you. People have been healed through prayer."

The couple came to see us, non-Christians but very nice people. We took them into our special "quiet room" to read the Scriptures, share with them, and pray for the wife as we laid our hands upon her. When they returned to their quarters the wife remarked to her husband that she felt at peace. The next day she said that she had been healed. There was no reason for them to return to the UK; he could finish his tour of duty. He reported this to the medical officer but arrangements were already in place so they still had to return to Britain.

After their move the wife told her husband that she was going to find a church and thank God for her healing. He wasn't sure about this. He was probably afraid she was going to get too religious! But he joined her and they attended an active evangelical Baptist church. They were both eventually born anew in Christ, baptized, and raised their family who all put their trust in the Lord. Some went into full-time service and are today doing missionary work. All of the grandchildren also love the Lord.

We knew nothing of all this until 2012, when I was

attending a men's breakfast meeting. The pastor spoke of how he had recently met this couple in another part of England, where he was conducting a series of Bible studies. Knowing he was from Reading, the couple approached him to ask if he knew us. He said he would be meeting me for only the second time in a few days, at the breakfast meeting where he was going to introduce me. The Lord is so gracious to encourage us to keep on going, sowing, seeking, and praying. We can leave the watering and reaping to Him!

Our most unexpected visitor to the centre came in 1973. A Christian brigadier general dropped by one day to inform us that her Royal Highness Princess Margaret was passing through Singapore on her way back to the United Kingdom. He wanted her to see the ministry of Sandes centres.

I was given a sheaf of instructions that detailed the correct protocol to follow for every moment I was in her royal presence. Soldiers came to lay down yards of green carpets so that her feet would not have to tread on ordinary grass. Then the great moment came: a car drew up and out stepped the princess.

Protocol promptly went out the window and I forgot everything. I simply extended my hand and gave Princess Margaret a warm welcome. The lady looked around but the hot, humid climate of Singapore was having its effect and she quickly sought a shady place to get some relief.

"How do you manage to do this Christian work year in and year out?" she asked me.

"It's by the grace of God, ma'am," I said.

"What do you say to the Roman Catholic soldiers in my regiment?"

"The same thing that I say to Protestant or atheist soldiers:

'Jesus said, "You must be born again."'

"What is your understanding of being born again?"

By this time the general and others of the entourage were clearly anxious to whisk the lady away. Yet she listened intently as I answered her question. Then she touched me on the sleeve and smiled. I had the inner conviction that she understood.

Altogether Edna and I spent almost fourteen years with Sandes, evangelizing the British military. We resigned only because we felt the Lord calling us to the island of Borneo, which is now divided among three countries, Malaysia and Brunei in the north, and Indonesia in the south.

I had gotten to know this third-largest island in the world and the work of the Borneo Evangelical Mission (BEM, which later merged with Overseas Missionary Fellowship or OMF) while visiting troops there by helicopter. As mentioned earlier, people in the jungles of Borneo were experiencing God in a dimension that I had never before witnessed. There had been people movements in the 1930s, with later outbreaks in the 1970s, in which whole tribes had turned to Christ. The gospel was spreading like wildfire from village to village and many miracles took place.

From the beginning, BEM's goal was to build a strong indigenous church by encouraging Bible translations into native languages and starting Bible schools. Leadership training also took place. This strategy fed the renewal and revival so the good news of Christ was continuing to spread to people living in the interior.

Four days before I left the UK for another ministry trip to Borneo I learned that a certain pastor in town had made an unfair remark about me. I had once been a member of the church. Some men who were present in the service told me what the minister had said and suggested that we meet with him. I declined, saying I was getting ready to go to Borneo and it didn't seem necessary. They were disappointed.

I arrived on the island and travelled several days upriver and into the mountains to meet with some of the tribal people. I stayed in a long house, a very extended wide space in which many families lived, common in that part of Southeast Asia. Like most of these wooden structures it was raised off the ground on stilts, and the space divided into a more or less public area along one side and a row of private living quarters lining the other side.

As I sat in the public area I noticed two old men in particular who were totally covered with tattoos – each one of them, I was told, representing a person they had killed in their head hunting days. Yet as they looked at me their love was evident, almost tangible. They smiled continuously as they chatted.

When I mentioned this, my translator smiled. He said these men had only been Christians for six months, and they loved me for coming among them to share Jesus. But, he added after further discussion with them, God had also revealed something particular about me to them.

I was intrigued. I asked the men what that was, expecting a compliment of some sort.

"God has given you a great heart of love," he translated. "But there is a stone in it, and unless the stone is taken out it will grow, and your heart will harden."

"I want to know what this stone is," I said.

"You have not forgiven a pastor who said something about you in the town you come from, and unless you do that, your heart will become hard."

I was dumbfounded. Only the Holy Spirit could have revealed an incident that took place seven thousand miles away, bringing it to light through babes in Christ.

"It is true," I admitted. "I told the men that spoke to me in England that what their pastor said didn't matter, but it did."

They said I needed to repent, and I knew I couldn't put it off. I repented right there and then, in front of everyone. If I needed any further evidence of God at work among these people, this was it. For the next three days I felt a special anointing in my preaching and teaching. My translator experienced a double anointing.

Edna and I felt the Lord was asking us to do everything we could to encourage the blossoming churches. There were periods that we lived in Singapore and used that country as our springboard, because the Islamic government in Borneo wouldn't give me a permanent visa. Through fundraising we were able to facilitate practical training and many evangelistic projects.

I also led teams and individuals into the interior to contribute medical care, and to catch the excitement of what was going on. On one occasion I took three earnest and well-educated Chinese men. With them was a personal friend and pastor from the UK. We were visiting a village one evening when everyone gathered to worship the Lord. The atmosphere was rich and powerful, pregnant with the sense of the divine among us. These people knew more of God than we did, and they didn't even have an alphabet or Scriptures in their own language. We had even observed children blessed with spiritual gifts, praying for the sick and seeing them healed.

Suddenly a woman who had a baby at her breast started to speak in a language that was completely unknown to this tribe. We knew what it was, because it was perfect English. The woman's face was aglow as she prophesied that God was going to do a new thing in this country and bring in a new administration to rule. At that time its government was almost completely dominated by Islam.

I shall never forget the shock this lady's words gave to my companions. They were astounded that the tribal people present did not know what she said. We asked the leaders how she could speak such perfect English. Had she ever had an education?

They shook their heads, as nonplussed as we were. The whole message had to be translated from English into the tribal dialect. When it was finally understood by the assembly, everyone lifted their voices in praise and glory to God.

Unsurprisingly, the following year, a new Christian native party was voted in and the Muslim government lost control. A decade of changes was ushered in.

4
INTO THE UNKNOWN

Within a few weeks after the confirmation of the prophecy we'd been given in 1986, both in Singapore and Ireland, a letter arrived from a friend in Lebanon. Lebanon was still affected by civil war so he was working with the Bible Society in Cyprus to get literature. We had known this man for years, and he had already shared our circumstances with the Bible Society director in Lebanon.

"We feel you and Edna would be the right people to join us," he wrote, "using Cyprus as a springboard to take God's Word in Arabic to the people of Syria, Lebanon, the Arabian Gulf, and all of the Arabian Peninsula. Will you come over and help us?"

Believing this invitation was of God, we took the letter to the pastor and elders of our church in Reading. The church sent us to Cyprus with their blessing.

After arriving at the Bible Society base in Larnaca and getting settled, I asked my new colleagues where I should start. I didn't speak a word of Arabic, but they said they believed I was called and the Lord would give me the right words at the right time.

"Which is the most difficult Arabic country to take God's Word?" I queried.

"That would be Saudi Arabia, of course." The response came without hesitation.

"Well then, I'll go there first!"

"It isn't as easy as that," explained the staff. "You have to have a contact – a sponsor – on the inside of the country to get a Saudi visa. That takes time."

"Fine. So what's the second most difficult place?"

They named another Middle Eastern nation where there was no Christian activity, no churches, and only tiny pockets of believers.

"Okay, I'll go there." After all, this was what God had commissioned me to do.

"Perhaps on this first trip you could take ten or twenty copies of the Bible in your luggage. It would be wonderful if you could get those in! The secret believers need them."

I thought about that. If I were to be caught and arrested for taking only twenty Bibles, why shouldn't I take two hundred? That was the beginning of my career as a courier, as related in the first chapter.

On my second trip to this same conservative country, my boxes of books were confiscated by customs. I went in search of the director of the airport, and when I found his office I saw a small boy sitting in one of the chairs. I addressed him gravely.

"Are you the director of the airport?"

Laughter erupted from behind the desk and a man said, "Maybe one day he will be. How can I help you?"

I explained that the custom officials had confiscated all my copies of the holy books of God that I had brought with me. Did he think that this was right?

"No," said the director. He wrote something down on a

piece of paper and stamped it before handing it to me. I am quite sure his kindness was due to the attention that I had paid to his little boy. I took the paper to customs. The officials were not pleased; however, I got my books.

On the third trip I decided to take even more Scriptures – three trolley loads of them! The trouble was, I only had one pair of hands, so I had to take two of the trolleys to customs and then go back for the third.

The customs men were absolutely furious. Again, they confiscated the Bibles, so I went back to the airport director and told him what had happened.

The man sighed. "It's difficult," he said.

"Difficult, sir?"

"Yes. Look through this window behind me. Do you see the sweeper? He is spying on me."

I exclaimed with surprise. "Spying on you?"

"Yes. I'm afraid you will have to go to the minister of censorship and the minister of information to get your books released. And if you do not you may have to go to the Sharia court. If you go there you may go to prison! I'm so sorry."

"That's all right, my friend," I told him. "Thank you."

I set off to look for the government buildings and the ministers I needed to talk to. Entering first the ministry of censorship I asked, "Tell me, sir, the holy books of God – the Torah, Zabur and Injil – are they censored in this country?"

"How can they be censored? In the Quran they are called the three Holy Books of Heaven. They cannot be censored! But we have to prevent them from entering."

At least he was honest about it. I said, "Well, I brought these holy books with me and I want to have them back."

"You will have to go to the ministry of information," the man told me.

I knew it was very difficult to gain an audience with any minister; usually you only get to see their secretaries. The only way to get past them is to look official; walk as if you know where you're going and you have an appointment.

I managed to see the minister. He wanted to talk about London and the night clubs there – it always amazed me that these "conservative" Muslims were all familiar with the night clubs – but eventually he released the books to me. I was thrilled. The Lord was so great!

I was finding that each time I entered that country there was one particular senior officer in customs who was very aggressive and difficult. I called him Mr Fanatic. I told Edna about him and when I was lining up my next trip I said, "This man is on duty in the morning, at lunch time, and in the evenings. He won't get me this time because I've got a ticket to land at midnight!"

Edna looked disturbed. "My dear Tom, I don't agree with you. You have moved from walking in the Spirit to leaning on the flesh. God is already doing miracles and you are now trying to engineer them yourself!"

I felt rebuked and repented of my actions, but told her I already had the ticket.

"Yes, I know, and I'll be on my knees. You know that."

The only reason I've been able to stay on my feet all these years is because I've had a wife on her knees. I prepared for my trip. Knowing I wouldn't be seeing Mr Fanatic this time, I decided to go for even more books – 300 kilos.

Coming off the midnight flight I grabbed some trolleys like everyone else, loaded my boxes, and headed for customs.

Guess who was on duty? I spotted him from a distance and said, "Lord, that's really not fair."

Mr Fanatic had also spotted me. He cried out, "No, no, NO!"

I said, "Yes, yes, yes!" and tried to be very polite, but he was nearly climbing the wall in his wrath.

"I told you before that we do not have Christians in our land!"

"I know that you do have Christians and these are their holy books, and they have every right to have them."

"I warned you," he spat at me. "These books will be destroyed and you will go to prison!"

At that moment there was a commotion behind him. An elegantly dressed Arab had walked into the terminal and the other customs officers were running over to him, reaching out their hands. The man graciously touched their fingers as he passed and came directly over to where I stood. He tapped Mr Fanatic's shoulder. When the officer saw who it was he started bowing obsequiously.

"*Salaam Alaikum!*" he cried. "Peace be unto you!"

The gentleman turned to me and asked in perfect Oxford English, "Do you have problems?"

"Yes, sir, I do. The officer here says that all my holy books will be destroyed, and I will go to prison!"

"Are they Holy Bibles?" he wanted to know.

It was most unusual for any Arab to use the word "Bible". Christians were said to use the Holy Book and were called "people of the Book".

I told him they were indeed Holy Bibles.

"What language are they in?"

"This trolley has Arabic copies, this trolley has Arabic

and Urdu, and this one has mixed languages.

He gave me a smile and directed, "Go through."

Mr Fanatic promptly exploded into a volley of protests but the gentleman raised a finger and he stopped. The stranger motioned for me to pass through the barrier. I went, rejoicing and praising God.

Contacts waited for me outside the airport in six cars. They loaded all the Bibles – apart from what I would be using – into their boots and went off in different directions.

Soon after that a German diplomat of my acquaintance, a very devout man of God, contacted me to say that he and his wife wanted me to come to his home for dinner. He was also inviting six other foreign diplomats for the evening.

"I want you to give your testimony, Tom, tell them how Jesus came into your life," he said.

I told him I was very willing to do that and went to his house at the appointed time.

"This is my friend Tom," my friend introduced me to the others who were already assembled. "Tom is a missionary and he carries the Word of God in Arabic."

"In Arabic!" one exclaimed. "Here?"

"Yes. Tell them about it, Tom," he urged. "Tell them what happened at the airport."

So I shared the incident about Mr Fanatic and the stranger who had intervened. Two of the diplomats looked at each other.

"We know who that was," said one.

"You do?"

"Yes! He's a member of the royal family in this country, and you never see him except on television, meeting VIPs like Prince Charles or a president or prime minister. We know he was at the airport that night."

"Well, he rescued me. Mr Fanatic was blue in the face but he got me through."

"Do you know why?" asked a diplomat. "When he was a boy he was sent from this country to a Christian mission school in another Muslim nation to learn English."

God's hand was obviously in that whole encounter. It was as if He had said to me, "Tom, my dear son, why didn't you listen to your wife? Now you are here and you're stuck – but I will bring someone along who is sympathetic to my Word."

I believe that member of the royal family truly was sympathetic. He may even have been a secret believer. You can imagine what a great encouragement his intervention was.

In several subsequent visits to that country, Mr Fanatic was not on duty. Neither was the director of the airport who had helped me.

When my consignment was again confiscated on the next trip I had to go to the minister of education, and he told me he couldn't help. This time I would have to appeal to the Sharia court. Conservative Muslim countries like this one are ruled by Islamic or Sharia law, which covers both public and private behaviour. Of all legal systems in the world today, Sharia law is surely among the most intrusive and strict.

I hailed a taxi and when the driver asked where I was going, I told him the Sharia court.

"Sharia?" he whispered, his eyes wide.

"Yes, please."

As the man drove he asked, "You are English? Go to Sharia? Not good."

He stopped outside a building and said this was it. The

place didn't look very imposing but he insisted he was right. I asked him to wait for me and went inside. Nobody was around so I opened another door and found men in chains along three of the walls, and two guards with rifles.

"Sorry!" I said and backed out hastily. Outside I told the taxi driver that this was the wrong place.

"It is Sharia prison! Like you ask!"

"I didn't ask for Sharia prison, but the Sharia court!"

I got back into the taxi and the driver took me to a lovely looking building with two guards standing outside. This was the place. I started to give the driver some money but he shook his head.

"No money!"

"What do you mean? You brought me a very long way. I am a Christian and I will pay you." I pressed the money into his hand. Then I strode purposefully past the guards, carrying my briefcase that contained about six Bibles and Gospels. I greeted the guards with a *Salaam Alaikum* and opened the door.

In front of me was a magnificent marble staircase. I didn't know which way to go so I went up the steps. At the top was a long corridor, and at the end of this were two men sitting at a desk. They stood as I approached. I knew they were going to ask me if I had an appointment, so I just said, *"Salaam Alaikum!* Is the president in?"

"Yes. Have you got an appoint –?"

"Thank you!" I said cheerily and opened the door.

One of the things I like about the Arab culture is that once people see you face-to-face, they can never turn you away. You can go to any Arab home and you will be welcomed. So I went into the chamber and found about twenty or twenty-five *mullahs*, educated in Islamic theology and sacred law. One man sat elevated above them on a platform, the president or *ayatollah*. There was only one empty seat so I sat down in it and waited for the president to beckon me forward. While I waited two young men entered the court wearing beautifully embroidered robes and gold on their fingers. Everyone immediately stood up to show their respect so I stood as well. The *ayatollah* came down to greet them by rubbing noses. Obviously these were very important people indeed!

The two youths went to sit with the chief. Coffee was brought for them and they talked for about twenty minutes. Then the president got back on his throne and looked at me. I was being summoned.

As I walked on that beautifully woven carpet with my briefcase I breathed a prayer against the spirit of Islam. The man indicated a chair and then leaned close, clenched his teeth, and hissed, "What do you want?"

I have no explanation for the words that came out of my mouth. In fact, my spirit rose up immediately after I spoke them to admonish, *What are you thinking of? What a dumb thing to say!* But Jesus has told us in His Word that God's Spirit will tell us what to say in our hour of need.

I asked the president of the court, "How is your father?"

I didn't even know if the man's father was alive! He might have been dead for years. But the president, clearly astonished, replied, "Thank you. He is beginning to make a recovery after his long illness."

The man's demeanour underwent a miraculous change.

He then asked, "What can I do for you?"

I explained that my holy books of God had been taken

from me at the airport, and the minister had told me I must come and see the president of the Sharia court.

"If you sign the paper, I can have the books back."

"Books?"

"The Torah, Zabur, and Injil."

"You brought Christian books into this country?"

The two young visitors sat riveted, at the edge of their seats.

I responded, "Of course I brought these books. Everyone has a right to hear the Word of God." I quoted from the Quran: "'… that the People of The Book (Bible) are to live according to the Injil (Gospel)'. Are not these the books he was talking of?"

"Ha! Muhammad the Prophet – peace be upon him – wrote the holy book. You people have corrupted God's words in your many versions."

He was really getting worked up.

"Sir," I said, "the word 'version' that is written on some Bibles is very unfortunate. It should read 'translation'. In our own culture we understand that 'version' means 'translation'."

I started going into the history of translation but the president's phone rang. He swivelled around to answer it while I studied the opulence all around me. Then my eyes caught those of the two young men who were smiling and nodding their heads, obviously signalling me to keep going.

The president finished his phone call, swivelled back to me and said, "I cannot talk to you now. I have two eminent visitors. Come back with your papers tomorrow. I will release the books."

"Do you guarantee that in the name of God?" I asked, knowing this man would never go back on his promise if he said those words.

"Yes, in the name of God."

"Thank you, sir. I apologize for the interruption and will come back tomorrow."

As I stood up to leave the court the young men stood up, so everyone else also rose. The pair came over to me and asked, "You are from England, aren't you?"

"Yes, I'm from England," I smiled.

"We were educated there. You are a man of the Book?"

"Yes, I am."

The older youth shook my hand. "It's been very nice to meet you. We wish you every success in what you are doing."

Startled, I thanked them and then left the courtroom. The next day, true to the president's word, my books were all returned to me.

Because I was not under contract as a businessman or oil worker it was always required of me, whenever I visited this country, to register at the British Embassy. I went there the day after my experience at the Sharia court, and the consul came to tell me that the ambassador wanted to see me. I followed him to the ambassador's office.

"Mr Hamblin. You know we've talked to you before and warned that one day you might have serious problems and land in prison," said the man. "You are breaking the law with what you're doing."

"No, sir," I replied. "I'm not technically breaking the law because I don't smuggle anything. I come here openly and declare what I bring openly. So I'm not breaking the law." I added, "You know that two British men were arrested for smuggling whisky a few weeks ago. You got them out of jail and sent them back to England. They broke the law. I have not."

"Yes, all right," acknowledged the ambassador. "But Mr Hamblin, there's one thing I want to ask you. How much longer will you be here? However long it is – and this is a very sensitive point for the British government – don't go anywhere near the Sharia court."

"I was there yesterday."

He stared at me. "You couldn't have been. No foreigner is allowed anywhere near it, including ambassadors."

"I'm sorry, but I was there."

"How did you get in?" he demanded.

"I walked in."

"And what happened?"

I described my experience, noting the presence of the two young men who had also been there, encouraging me as I had a bit of a tussle with the president of the court.

"They shook my hand when I left," I finished.

The ambassador and the consul looked at each other. The former picked up the daily Arabic newspaper, and there on the front page was a photo of the two young men and the Sharia court.

"Were these the –"

"Yes!" I interrupted with an exclamation. "Those are the very young men I met, who wished me well! Who are they?"

"They are two princes of the royal family."

I was still digesting this fact when the ambassador asked me to tell him what happened in regard to my request to the president.

"I got all my Bibles back," I told him.

Over the five years and three months that I went in and out of this country I continually experienced God breaking bars of iron, as He had promised to do.

I was able to build up quite a nice relationship with the minister of information. On my fourth visit "Fanatic" was on duty again, and again he confiscated all my Bibles. I was advised to go to the minister of information, who asked, "You bring the Christian Holy Book?" I said yes. "This time I'll sign for them. When will you be returning?" I told him I visited about every three months.

He said, "I want you to do something, Mr Thomas. Every time you're planning to come I want you to fax or email me and tell me how many Arabic, Persian, English, Urdu, and other Bibles you are bringing, and I'll okay it. Here's my card with the number. You won't have any trouble when you arrive."

I thanked him warmly. I was so excited I could hardly wait for the next three months to pass. When the time came I sent a fax to the minister, listing the Bibles I was bringing and giving him my flight details.

After I landed I stood with other passengers in the arrivals area, waiting for my boxes and baggage to come through. Then an Arab in flowing robes strode over.

"Mr Thomas? We've been expecting you," he told me. The luggage belt started up at that moment, and the first items to appear from the plane were all my boxes! No stamps or marking on them, no delays. I just loaded my trolleys and sailed through the exit!

My friends were jubilant. The next time I went to the government office to thank the minister I was allowed into his office. No one warned me that he had two other ministers with him. I sat down while they carried on talking in Arabic. Finally he said to the other two men, in English, "Do you know who this Englishman is? Have you not seen him before? He is a holy man of God. He brings the Holy Book."

And then this same nice, friendly man turned to me and yelled, "And what about Salman Rushdie?"

"Salman Rushdie?" I echoed. "Didn't he write a book?"

"You *know* he wrote a book, and you English people – you Westerners – read his filthy lies."

I looked him in the eye. "Because I am a Christian, I read the holy Injil which tells me not to read Salman Rushdie's book."

He was astonished. "Are you saying your Injil says you must not read this book?"

"Yes," I replied, and reached into my briefcase for an Arabic/English New Testament. I opened to Philippians 4:8 and read aloud:

Finally, brothers and sisters, whatever is true, whatever is noble, whatever is right, whatever is pure, whatever is lovely, whatever is admirable – if anything is excellent or praiseworthy – think about such things.

"You see," I added, "that's why I've never read Salman Rushdie's book, and why I will never read it."

"Those are lovely words," exclaimed the minister. "They are in the Injil?"

"Oh yes, and many more words like them."

"Read them again!"

So I read the verses again, and after the second reading I said, "Sir, would you like one of these holy books of God? I have a copy in English or Arabic."

"I would like it in Arabic," he responded.

The other two cabinet ministers spoke up. "Do you have any more?"

Before leaving the office, I thanked the minister of information for helping me get my Bibles through customs.

"You are welcome," he said, and then added, "But the next time you come, *don't fill up the aircraft!*"

On what turned out to be my final visit to this country my book boxes were once again confiscated, and this time I was put in detention for three days. Fortunately, although I wasn't allowed any of my other personal luggage, the officials gave me my briefcase and never even looked inside. I always carried some Gospels in that briefcase.

The Lord gave me a good congregation while I was in that detention cell. Every prisoner got a Gospel. One of the men was named Tawoomi, a black African Muslim wearing a traditional head cap and robes. I asked him why he was behind bars.

"The Muslims here are not nice," he shook his head sadly. "In my village they collected money to send me to Jordan to train to become a *mullah* (priest). When I got to Jordan I showed my papers and told authorities I was there to study. They said, 'No, you're not.' In some Muslim countries they don't like black-skinned people. So they put me on a plane that landed here, and I was put in detention."

I said, "God has His purposes."

I opened my Bible and we began to read it together. We kept on until four or five the next morning when I told Tawoomi that I needed to sleep. He was still reading the Scriptures avidly a few hours later when I woke up, feeling refreshed. I asked my new friend how much a ticket would cost to his homeland.

"A lot of money," he answered gloomily. "A hundred and ninety dollars."

I had in my pocket two one-hundred dollar bills. It was all I had, but I felt the Holy Spirit telling me to give the bills to Tawoomi. I told him this and he began to cry.

"It's Jesus," he said. I agreed.

He told the officers he had the money and left the detention area. I admit that I couldn't help privately wondering, "Could I have the ten dollars change, Lord?" Tawoomi wasn't able to come back and see me but I caught a glimpse of him as he was being led off. He waved and mouthed the name "Jesus"! I never saw him again.

The chief of detention said I was in trouble, and wanted to know why I had given the money away. "Jesus," I told him. I was eventually released and ordered to take a British Airways flight to London.

"But I don't live there," I objected. "I live in Cyprus!"

They wouldn't listen and I was conducted onto the plane, unshaven and scruffy. The airline attendant informed me, "We've been waiting for you!" Everyone on board wanted to know what I'd done.

I asked to speak to the captain. He came back to where I sat and shook my hand.

"I'm not a religious man myself," he admitted.

I answered, "Neither am I, but I am a committed Christian."

I asked him if there was a chance the plane could stop in Bahrain on the way out.

"It just so happens that we've been asked to stop in Bahrain," replied the captain, adding, "I've been told by the authorities to take you back to London. Usually that means you're a *persona non grata* [the label given by a government to a foreigner whose entering or remaining in their country is prohibited]."

Nevertheless, the captain landed and even waited to see if I'd made it safely through immigration. I told the officials at the desk that I only planned to stay two or three days and then return to Cyprus. They gave me thirty days! I had no money – not even a credit card at that time. So I asked a stranger for a few coins to call local friends. My friends were startled to hear from me and thought I was calling from Cyprus, but they came for me and I stayed with them and got cleaned up.

I was walking down the street when I ran into a big American fellow who was working at the mission hospital in Bahrain.

"Tom Hamblin!" he hailed me joyfully. "At last! God told me weeks ago to put two hundred dollars in my shirt pocket for you. Whenever I changed my shirt I put the money back in the new one."

I told this brother my story and the big guy's eyes filled with tears.

A few days later another friend who also happened to be an airline pilot took me back to the Bahrain airport, using a behind-the-scenes route. There we discovered all my boxes of Bibles that had been confiscated and loaded onto the BA flight when I boarded. The captain must have seen to it that they were unloaded when I disembarked. My pilot friend's eyes opened wide when he saw them, and we both gave glory to the Lord. He arranged for the boxes to travel back to Cyprus with me.

That was the last of twelve visits I was able to make to that country, and although that particular consignment of books didn't reach their intended readers, I was able to take in at least two and a half thousand kilos of Scriptures that did make it.

Cyprus served as our base for a total of almost sixteen years. After the first three with the Bible Society we were accepted under the umbrella of OM International, whose members are expected to depend entirely on God and His people to meet their expenses. Edna and I discovered we did better living by faith than by having a regular salary! The Lord honours all who walk with Him in obedience.

5
THE ENTRANCE OF YOUR WORD

The Bible Society of Lebanon, from its office and very large store in Cyprus, was able to send thousands of Bibles, New Testaments, and other books into the Arab world. But only in three countries was it legally allowed to import Scriptures. Supplies of literature for the rest of the Muslim nations needed to be hand-carried to their intended destinations, especially if they were in specific languages.

During the three years that Edna and I served with the Bible Society of Lebanon I enjoyed the companionship of David Mitchell from New Zealand. What a positive attitude David had! In answer to every difficult situation that arose he would always declare, "No problem." On one occasion he and I openly travelled to a large country in the Arabian Peninsula with five thousand Arabic Bibles, Injils, and children's Bibles.

"You can't do that!" some well-meaning friends in Cyprus advised. "You'll never get them through!"

We persevered in what we felt was God's direction, however, and all the boxes passed safely through customs. Within a month we had distributed those precious books throughout the land.

I remember one remarkable experience in particular. We had loaded a vehicle with Scriptures and gone deep into the heart of the country, travelling hour after hour across the desert. David said to me, "Tom, we are now running on vapour. The petrol tanks are empty! Better get praying, man of God."

I did pray as he continued to drive. We kept going.

Suddenly in the shimmering desert heat we saw an oil well in front of us. I wondered at first if it was a mirage but it was the real thing all right, and alive with workers. When we reached the operation we went into the main office and found a group of men from the Netherlands. They were amazed to see us, and enquired why we were in "no man's land". When we told them we were carrying Bibles, and asked if we could use a table in their canteen to display them, they appeared shell-shocked.

"No one reads the Bible here," one man finally responded. However, they gave us permission and we gifted each of them with Scriptures in English. As the employees on the rig left their work and entered the canteen, David and I stood by our large table display and started to engage the men in conversation.

One Arab called out to his friends, "Come here! Come here! These books are the Torah, Zabur, and Injil, which I read in England when I was in training. This is the true Injil! You must each get one!"

They all willingly accepted copies, but the Arab who had first spoken asked for six copies to give to his family and friends.

The Dutch staff made sure we left with a tank full of petrol, food, and cold drinks. It was an awesome opportunity. We sowed so many Scriptures at that oil well that we had to replenish our supplies, which meant returning to our friends who stored them in the passageway of their home.

We found that one of the best places to distribute Scriptures is petrol stations. When I drove in there were always Muslim attendants: Arabs or Pakistanis or Bengalis. I would get out and talk with them and ask if they had ever read an Injil. They always responded that Injils weren't available in their country. Then I'd pull one out and they'd marvel and exclaim with excitement. As other cars arrived, their drivers also got excited.

Cafés also offered opportunities. Whenever we had a chance for a cup of tea after driving in the desert for hours, we took it. Once we sat in a café with our tea and an Injil on the table. The Pakistani man who had served us lingered.

"Excuse me, sir," he said, "are you working here on a contract?"

"No, I work for a king. Can you guess which king it is?"

"It must be Jesus," he stated.

I asked why he would say that. He replied some of the best schools back home were Christian schools, and he had been sent to one as a boy.

"Would you like to have a Bible in your language, Urdu?" I then asked him.

"You have one in this country?" he exclaimed. He followed me out to the car and when he saw the Arabic Bibles he asked if he could have one in Arabic as well. I asked why, and he explained that many Arabs asked him if he knew how to get the book of Jesus.

"I respond to them, 'How would I know, I'm a Pakistani!'"

So I gave him some Arabic copies too. He might sell them, but I didn't care. Pakistanis are brilliant business people!

When David and his energetic, no-nonsense wife Susan

eventually left Cyprus to return to New Zealand we felt a great vacuum. But we pressed on.

* * *

My first visit to Lebanon was in 1986, when I was still working with the Bible Society. Bordered by Syria to the north and east and Israel to the south, Lebanon's rich history encompasses about seven thousand years. It is the only Arab country not officially Muslim and there is freedom of religion. However, mistrust between Muslims and Christians is deeply ingrained. Sectarian tensions boiled over into a sixteen-year civil war in 1975, resulting in massive loss of human life and property and devastating the country's economy.

My fellowship with the staff members was extremely positive, even though the fighting between different factions was still raging. So many thousands of innocent people had lost their lives, their homes, and their businesses. Evangelicals felt particularly threatened since they numbered less than 1 per cent of the population and weren't even well accepted by other traditional Christian groups. Yet the mandate of the Lebanon Bible Society was to distribute the Word of God equally to one and all. I admired the courage of all of the staff, but some individuals in particular showed a special boldness from the Spirit of God. Many people would call their actions foolhardy, but in their view they were simply acting in obedience to the One who gave them the Spirit of love and power. They reflected a deep compassion for all segments of society.

One such worker was blessed with the same first name as me! Tom was married to a lovely lady named Anna and they had three delightful children. The family lived in a mountain area that was regarded as comparatively safe. They offered me accommodation, which I gladly accepted.

The children had gone to bed that first evening and we three were sharing fellowship together, enjoying getting to know each other, when bombs suddenly started to fall near the house. That was enough for Tom and Anna to awaken the children from their sleep and wrap them in blankets. Then each of us carried a child as quickly as possible down the mountain to a place of safety.

I can remember how their house shook that night, and looking across the ravine and seeing the tracer fire of bullets in both directions, emitting a bright glow against the sky. It all seemed surreal. Yet I kept assuring myself in wonder, *This is not a video. This is real warfare going on around us, and people are very likely being killed.*

Later, Tom and I experienced some good times travelling over the country in a transit vehicle, transporting the Word of God to where it was most needed. One day we saw some Syrian soldiers who had crossed the border into Lebanon and set up road blocks. We were forced to stop so Tom, bold as a lion, greeted the soldiers warmly. The two men at the checkpoint began to smile at whatever he was saying. I didn't have a clue as to what that was, since I didn't know Arabic. However, Tom gave them a New Testament and they called out to their fellow soldiers who were on a nearby rise. I did catch the word "Injil", for the men repeated it, and suddenly one after the other was sliding down the slopes, stirring up a cloud of sand dust. With big smiles they each reached out to take a copy of the Gospel in Arabic. I couldn't say exactly how many we handed out that day, but it was a good number. We left the soldiers elated at their possession of Scriptures and we, too, gave joyful thanks to God as we travelled on. What an encouragement to see this brother in action, serving God without fear in a war zone.

Another man was very much like Tom in boldness, although he was quieter. "Job" was from the Netherlands but loved the Muslim people and deeply desired them to know the Lord Jesus personally. At the time I met him he was unmarried, but he has now been wed for a number of years to a lady who matches him in vision. They have children and remain living among the Lebanese people, earning their love and loyalty in return.

Job invited me to accompany him for some literature distribution in the east of Beirut, known to be the Shia[2] side. He took along a large folding table and plenty of Arabic Bibles and New Testaments, as well as some children's Bible stories. As Westerners we stood out among the crowds of Muslim Lebanese.

However, we erected the tables beside a favourite seaside promenade and soon people gathered around us. They obviously took a keen interest in the literature and asked questions which only my friend could answer in Arabic. All I could do in those days was smile and pray silently as I held a Bible or New Testament in my hands for them to see. Some passers-by wanted to buy the books. The price was minimal so a great many could afford them. All seemed to be going well until a Muslim policeman appeared in the crowd.

"What is this? What are you doing here?" he demanded, belligerently pushing a few people away from the table. He

2 Shia or Shiites and Sunnis represent the two main branches of Islam. Shiites believe that Islam should be led by descendants of Muhammad, while Sunnis (who are by far in the majority) believe that the leader of Islam should be appointed by election and consensus. There is often a great deal of tension between the two factions.

looked straight at Job, who didn't bat an eye but smiled at the man, greeting him softly. He explained what we were doing, then opened the Scriptures to the third chapter of John. Pointing to verses sixteen and seventeen, he asked the policeman to read them.[3]

The crowd stood quietly and listened as the officer read aloud. The silence was pregnant with interest. Although my eyes were open my heart was praying fervently to Abba Father, asking Him to open the spiritual eyes of these people.

When the policeman finished reading the verses it was evident that his attitude had completely changed. He even said something complimentary to us. Job offered him a copy as a gift, which he took with thanks, kissed it reverently, and walked away. Immediately the others crowded around and reached for the Scriptures. We sold out completely and said we would return the next day.

Sadly, however, we were unable to fulfil this promise because the fighting was so fierce we could not get through. No doubt the streets would have been emptied of people anyway.

* * *

I was happy to make many visits to this nation that was called the "Switzerland of the Middle East" until fighting and widespread destruction kept most visitors away. While the famous cedars of Lebanon are now few and far between, this is still the most densely wooded of all Middle Eastern countries. Looking down from pine-scented mountains

---

3 "For God so loved the world that he gave his one and only Son, that whoever believes in him shall not perish but have eternal life. For God did not send his Son into the world to condemn the world, but to save the world through him."

one is treated to a spectacular view of the Mediterranean coastline that blossoms with fruit trees and flowers during the summer. I am so pleased that a degree of normality has now been restored and the lovely seaport of Beirut has been rebuilt.

Before one of OM's "Love Lebanon" outreaches that I took part in, we were warned that it would be unwise to take the gospel to Muslims. Our team had thirty-five young people aged fifteen to thirty-eight, mostly composed of Lebanese, Jordanians, and a few Europeans. So we focused on the Druze people in mountain villages, who are considered to be followers of an offshoot of Shia Islam but with their own close-knit community and distinctive beliefs. We distributed English/Arabic New Testaments door-to-door, determined to accept any opposition for Christ's sake.

Six team members were taken for questioning by the police but afterwards released. Another day as we visited houses two by two, we saw two of our number approached by a Syrian officer and led away. Later we found out that this was a three-star general who had seen us talking to people on the street. He just wanted to invite the pair for coffee and a talk. They spent over an hour with him before he finally affirmed, "I know that Jesus is the King. Please give me an Injil." They handed one to him and then he asked for two more, to give to fellow officers.

Every day we experienced the Lord's presence. We held open-air meetings, although these had never before been tried and were considered dangerous. Hundreds stood listening – not for just five or ten minutes but for two hours at a time. English speakers had to be translated, of course. When I gave an invitation to those who wanted the assurance of knowing Abba Father, thirty stepped out in one meeting alone.

The only problems we encountered were with Maronites who belonged to the largest Christian denomination in the country, part of the Catholic Church. They kept asking us, "Do you worship Mary?" We said that we respected Mary but only Jesus could give eternal life. They were the only ones to refuse the Arabic language Bibles we distributed, and once poured lighter fluid over a Bible in order to set it on fire. All other people received God's Word with gladness and reverence.

I felt the Lord wanted me to share those words of life with the desert Bedouins, who are at the bottom of the social ladder, and invited my pastor from the UK, named Dave, to go with me. Some scoffed, "They can't read. Why go to them?" But when we found a few Bedouins on horseback they were excited over the Injil and sat on their mounts reading it. Then they urged us to eat with them. We spent three precious days in their community, talking until we were exhausted. Then a chief of police came along.

"Gentlemen, you've been giving away a book these past days," he observed in beautiful English. "What is it?"

"It's the Injil," I explained, "the holy Word of God. Would you like a copy?"

"Are you giving this to me?" he exclaimed in disbelief.

"Yes, take it. It's a gift."

He took the book and kissed it. "I am amazed by Christian history. When you think of the Reformation, Martin Luther, the martyrs of the faith…"

The policeman and my pastor started talking about Christian history and had a wonderful time.

"Which university did you attend?" Dave wanted to know. "Did you study in Britain?"

"I've been to no university. I've never left this country. I'm self-taught. But I'm an avid reader and I love Christian history. For the last two years I've asked God, 'Please, will you send me the Torah, the Zabur, and the Injil?' And now you have brought me the Injil!"

I delved into my bag and produced a complete Bible in Arabic. "Here is the rest!" I handed it over with a smile.

"Oh, my prayer is answered!" He stood there in awe holding the Injil and Bible. I was waiting for him to return the Injil but he asked, "Please may I keep the Injil too? I know another police officer who is very interested in Jesus."

I marvelled. It's not very often you get a Muslim police officer to do Scripture distribution!

"Before you leave," added this chief of police, "you must make me a promise. If you ever come back, you must find me and speak to me some more."

Pastor Dave returned to England after two weeks, overflowing with joy over the spiritual responsiveness he had seen in Lebanon.

During the war between North and South in this country, the OM team engaged in a mercy operation among Shia communities in the South, providing blankets, medicines, and food parcels to people displaced during the heavy bombings. Along with each parcel they gave an Arabic New Testament. Over four thousand homes gladly received them. The icing on the cake was that Hezbollah (a militant Islamist group and political party) actually escorted the team members for protection, even handing out the Scriptures and urging people to read them!

One man on the team met a very old Shiite Muslim and gave him some food. Then he offered an Arabic Bible. The man's reaction was very emotional and he started to cry. He could hardly speak for a few minutes. Then he reached inside his cloak and held up to the worker a faded, fragile copy of a booklet that he had with him, called "The Uniqueness of Christ".

This small booklet had been given to him twenty-three years before, the old man explained. He read it on the same day he received it, and believed that Jesus was the Son of God and Saviour of the world.

The man had prayed daily through the following years that one day he would have the Torah, Zabur, and Injil – the complete Bible. His prayer had at last been answered. The OM worker, deeply moved, prayed with this faithful believer before moving on.

* * *

Later it became essential for Edna and me to sever official ties with the Bible Society so that we could move Scriptures more freely into the Muslim countries of the Arab World. We were already known by many missions, and one group in particular, Operation Mobilisation (OM International), invited us under their wing. This allowed us accountability and transparency along with the liberty to obey the leading of God's Spirit.

We were so grateful to the Lord for opening this door. Living by faith alone, we looked to Him to provide the funds we needed to purchase large quantities of His Word for sowing and distributing in the Arabian Gulf and North Africa. We also helped to supply dozens of others working among immigrants in Europe and the United Kingdom.

Word had got around that an English couple living in Cyprus were distributing thousands of kilos of Scriptures, mostly in Arabic, Farsi, Urdu, Tagalog, French, and English – and they were free! Some assumed that OM provided the literature, but although they did contribute quantities this amount was in fact minimal compared with what we had to finance ourselves. We were being inundated with requests from many places for more Scriptures. I said to Edna that we needed at least £15–20,000 to supply the needs.

We received a phone call from an English couple whom we did not know, asking if they could spend an hour with us as they were passing nearby. We met them, had lovely fellowship, and they went on their way. God witnessed to them that we should have part of an inheritance, and they sent us a cheque for £40,000, which abundantly supplied all the Scriptures needed, and more!

The Bible Society gave us generous prices knowing that we were *sowing* rather than selling their literature. We bought most of the Arabic from a unique Bible publisher and distributer in the USA called the International Bible Society (IBS). This organization was always accommodating and their dual language Arabic/English Bibles and New Testaments were incredibly popular. Later the IBS also published an Arabic/French Bible, another winner. I would love to go to America one day and personally thank the society for their contribution.

I must also mention the MECO Mission – Middle East Christian Outreach – and its Bible and book ministry based in Cyprus for the entire Middle East. We purchased a lot of stock from them at favourable discounts, and they were always genuinely thrilled that the Lord was sending out His Word from their "storehouse".

Altogether we needed to raise an average US$100,000 per year to purchase Scriptures that were requested in various languages, and some years much more. Added to this was the cost of sending consignments by air cargo or post or, when necessary, carrying them in our own luggage to over fifteen countries. We took in several thousand kilos by hand over the years.

In return we received countless letters of thanks from the men and women who safely received this precious seed. One note was written by a pastor in Chad, a landlocked country in Central Africa where Muslims number over half the population. He reported that his consignment was being sown thick and fast, including the cassette tapes we had obtained from MECO. One man, descended from a long line of *mullahs*, had been converted through reading God's Word and listening to the tapes. Fifteen others of his family and friends also embraced Christ and were baptized secretly at four o'clock one morning. The pastor quoted verses 35 to 38 from Psalm 107, glorying in the greatness of our God:

> He turned the desert into pools of water and the parched ground into flowing springs; there he brought the hungry to live, and they founded a city where they could settle. They sowed fields and planted vineyards that yielded a fruitful harvest; he blessed them, and their numbers greatly increased, and he did not let their herds diminish.

Besides delivering literature to other sowers, I constantly had the joy of personally distributing the Word of life in unexpected places. I was in Kuwait City before the invasion of Iraq in 1990, walking down the street with my transparent bags of Bibles and asking God where I should go. Like other oil-rich parts of the Arab world, the city had blossomed into an impressive, modern metropolis, crowded with skyscrapers and yachts moored in the Persian Gulf.

I passed a large, elegant dress shop and could see a lot of veiled women inside. Muslim ladies love to wear colourful dresses underneath their all-encompassing black *abayas*; the younger ones often wear jeans. A sign outside the shop said "Women Only".

At that moment I clearly heard the Spirit of God telling me to go inside.

"Lord, it's a women's shop!" I objected. "I'm not allowed to mix with women here; it's impossible to speak to them!"

The Spirit persisted, however, and suddenly the electric doors opened without anyone near enough to trigger them. I obviously had no choice.

I went inside and immediately saw two lovely Filipina girls at the cash desk. They asked brightly if I wanted to buy a dress for my wife. I said no, she already had too many, which made them laugh.

"Then why are you here, sir?"

"I've come to ask you girls, do you love Jesus?"

They eagerly replied that they had met the Lord in the Philippines, just before coming to Kuwait, but had been instructed not to bring any Bibles or they would be sent home. I told them I could get copies for them, in either English or Tagalog. Then I asked if they had found a Filipino Christian fellowship. They hadn't, so I offered to find one for them to attend.

I was just turning to leave when one of the young women asked, "Do you have a Bible in Arabic?"

"Why do you want Arabic?"

She explained, "When Arab ladies come to buy from us they sometimes lean close and whisper, 'Do you have the book of Jesus [Isa]? Can you get one for me?' A number of them have asked."

I gave the girls ten kilos. They quickly put the Bibles behind the counter and I made them promise they would not distribute any books unless someone specifically asked for one.

Two days later I was back with two more bags of Bibles, including two in the Tagalog language for the girls, and they were thrilled. I also told them about a Tagalog fellowship they could attend in the city.

"Have you given out any of the Injils that I left?" I asked.

"Oh, yes." They led me around the counter and showed me my bag. It was nearly empty; only two or three copies remained of the thirty or forty I had given them!

"Did the ladies ask for all of those?"

"Yes!"

"Do you want more?"

"Oh, yes!" they exclaimed, so I left another ten kilos. The pair also showed me a list they had made of other shops where their friends worked, and where Muslim ladies were asking for Injils. In the next days I visited all these shops, and supplied the shop assistants with many Scriptures.

Back in Cyprus, when I shared this incident with our church, some members objected.

"Why give Muslim women Scriptures when most of them can't read?"

"Well," I reasoned, "how is it that the women in that city can drive cars if they can't read the road signs?"

While they thought about that, I added, "Even if they can't read, perhaps their husbands are asking for Bibles. Whichever way it is, praise God that they're asking for them!"

It always blows my mind when I get negative remarks like that from Christians, even from other missionaries. I remember one particular American missionary who wanted to come with David Mitchell and I on a distribution trip. We were giving out Scriptures in bus stations and garages and even outside mosques, and finally this missionary said, "I can't go on. You'll get us all arrested!"

I said, "You've been a missionary for nearly thirty years in this region. How many Muslims have you seen converted?"

"We just have to live our Christian lives before them. You can't be so overt in your witness."

"You must be overt if you want to convert," I stated firmly. "You are bound by fear, and God hasn't given us the spirit of fear."

This man had meant to stay with us for thirty days, but he left after only five.

I do understand that it is more difficult for workers who are living in the region and not just visiting it for a few weeks. But fear of losing one's place or position can creep in all too easily. I believe it is the right of every person – irrespective of who they are – to hear the gospel truth. They deserve it.

* * *

The invasion of Kuwait, also known as the Persian Gulf War, began in the early hours of 2 August 1990, when Saddam Hussein ordered more than 100,000 Iraqi troops across the border in tanks, helicopters, and trucks. Iraq had the fourth largest military force in the world. Saddam was confident that he could easily overwhelm his tiny Gulf neighbour and use its rich oil revenues to pay his debts.

What he didn't count on was the international response. The invasion was universally condemned, and coalition forces from thirty-four nations liberated Kuwait at the end of February 1991. Five days after Iraqi troops left Kuwait City in haste, I returned to that country. I told Edna I wanted to take five thousand Arabic Bibles and New Testaments, because they were so much needed.

We packed them up and I managed to find free carriage on a military aircraft. As this plane came in for landing we could see hundreds of oil wells that had been set on fire by the Iraqis, still burning. The airport had been mostly destroyed. As we rolled our loaded five or six trolleys of books to the customs area an official met us and asked, "Americana?"

"No," I said, "Britannia."

He beamed. "Ah, my friend, Mrs Thatcher's Number One, you go through!"

"Thank you, my friend!" I exclaimed. I felt like writing to Mrs Thatcher and thanking her. The Prime Minister's active opposition to Iraq's invasion and her mobilization of international support had obviously won Kuwaiti hearts. I had never before experienced such a welcome.

But I grieved at the state of this once-beautiful city. Everything had been totally ransacked by the invading troops, and what couldn't be carried away was destroyed. The pollution from the smoke of burning oil wells was terrible; you could taste it even through the air vents in the cars.

A few days after my arrival I was walking down one of the wide main streets carrying two bags with 10 kilos of Bibles in each of them, doing personal evangelism, when suddenly I heard someone shout, "Hello! Hello, Mr Injil man!"

I stopped in my tracks. There across the street was a man waving with both arms and grinning broadly. He came running across.

"Remember me, Mr Injil man?"

He must have realized by my blank expression that I didn't, so he proceeded to remind me that I had spoken to him before the Iraqi invasion, and given him an Arabic New Testament.

"Oh, my friend, my friend. Me and my family had to go into hiding during the occupation, for the Iraqis were terrible. We needed help so we started to read the Injil. It is so lovely! Isa saved us. We read the book many times."

He called me "*habibi*", an affectionate term only used between men who are real friends.

"I need the Torah and Zabur," he said urgently. "Please, can you give me?"

"Yes, of course I can. Here is a copy," I said, pulling a complete Arabic Bible from my bag. I kissed it reverently before handing it over.

The man was ecstatic and gave praise to God. Then he said, "I need six copies, please... No, eight, for all my family."

I enjoyed seeing him carry the books away with his chin resting on the top copy. As he left he shouted his thanks, "*Shukran, shukran, habibi!*" while I gave God the glory. Remembering the verse in Psalm 119:130, "The unfolding of your words gives light," I prayed that his whole family would come to believe in Jesus, the light of the world.

Later, as I was putting my bags through a security scanner at a bank I heard another man nearby exclaim, "You are the Injil man! Before the invasion you gave me an Injil. You must come and eat with me!"

I thanked him and said I'd be glad to.

Suddenly he added, "But why – why did you stab Mrs Thatcher in the back?"

That threw me. I assumed he was referring to the ousting of the Prime Minister by the Conservative Party, and assured the man that I hadn't stabbed her personally.

Everyone was still on edge from the war and I was stopped even as I approached hotels carrying my bags. As I wondered how to distribute my huge consignment of Bibles most effectively, I heard from an American pastor in the city. Jerry and Jacquie Zandstra had served in Kuwait before the invasion and remained many years after. Under God's direction they had built up the church and seen great numbers added. Several different language groups held services in the same building. This couple had servants' hearts and they had made a big impact on me.

Jerry said the US military was offering him the chance to distribute large warehouses-full of thousands of tonnes of American food. There was so much poverty in the city, tens of thousands of hungry people on the streets, without work. The US didn't want to just leave their supplies behind unsupervised since they were pulling out, with Kuwait now liberated.

"How would it be if I put up a few tables and offered Bibles in Arabic on one side, as you give out food on the other side?" I suggested. "There would be no pressure for people to take them."

Jerry thought it was a great idea. "We can feed them physically and spiritually," he enthused.

Throngs of desperate people queued up at the distribution point on the appointed day. As they collected the food they looked longingly over at the boxes of Bibles we had piled up on two tables.

"Oh... the Injil! But we have no money," they sighed. I got somebody to translate and told them that every family could have one free, if they wished. They were overjoyed. Two thousand copies of God's Word went into the eager hands of two thousand Muslim families. Our loving Father arranged it all.

In Iraq, too, the demand for God's Word accelerated through troubled times. By 1997 the hunger exceeded all expectations, and two ministries based in Jordan were officially allowed to take several thousands of Bibles and New Testaments into Iraq for a book exhibition and school visits. We sent a few thousand of our stock in Cyprus to help, and covered the cost of five thousand copies for students.

Yet delivering much smaller quantities into the hands of individuals was no less rewarding. I remember cycling into the countryside one hot afternoon during the period that Edna and I were doing reconstruction work on the church property in Aden, Yemen. I had tied two strong plastic bags over the handlebars of my old bicycle that mostly contained Arabic Bibles and New Testaments, as well as a few English and French language versions.

The sun blazed down from a cloudless sky as I approached the main gates of an oil company. It was so quiet I wondered if anyone was working or if all the employees were sleeping somewhere in the shade. But then I noticed a security guard sitting on a plastic chair and with a handkerchief over his head, reading a book. We greeted each other and I asked him what book he was so engrossed in.

"It's a Quran," he replied. We got talking about our families and how many children we had. I told him that Edna and I had two, a son and a daughter. He proudly said that Allah had given him ten sons (I noticed he left his wife out of the equation).

Then we got on to the Quran. After listening to the man advocate its virtues I remarked, "Well, I have read the Torah, Zabur, and Injil, and I love the Word of God."

The guard's next question was so sincere that his face lit up. "Oh, have you got a copy of the true Injil for me?"

I took out a nicely designed Arabic New Testament and offered it to him. He took the Book with great pleasure and kissed it reverently. His next words, explaining that he regularly listened to Arabic Christian radio programmes, put a lump in my throat.

"A good number in my village believe in Isa and the Injil more than the Quran," he added. "There are only a few Qurans in the village, and no Injils."

"Would you like to take one of my bags of Bibles and Injils?"

The man leapt up from his chair and hugged me tight, then kissed me on both cheeks (I always wished that Arab men shaved more regularly). At length he opened the security gates to let me through.

Inside the oil company office a Canadian friend told me he had observed my exchange with the guard and could tell I was "sowing the seed"; however, I should be careful because not everyone was in favour of my overt witnessing. I gave him the same reply I had given my missionary friend above: "You have to be overt to convert." He agreed and said I wasn't like so many others who hide their light under a bucket.

I was able to make later visits to this place, and as a direct result of the guard introducing me to others, many more men asked for copies of the Injil.

A Dutch Christian acquaintance who was working for an oil company in another country (I will refrain from saying exactly where) once asked me how I distributed Bibles. After I explained my usual methods he said, "I wonder, I have a day off soon. Can I go with you somewhere into the interior?"

I was delighted to agree to his proposal, especially since he had an air-conditioned vehicle with a four-wheel drive. So we drove into the mountains and got out, filled our backpacks with books, and started to climb. As we came over the first high hill we saw five men climbing up towards us from the valley below, where there was a village with a mosque.

When the men spotted us they greeted us with excitement, "*Salaam Alaikum*! We have never had white people visit us. You are the first! Why do you come?" "I'll tell you why," I said, reaching into my backpack. "We have come with the holy Injil of Isa."

"The true Injil?"

"Yes. The true Injil, from God."

All the men were keen to have one and they thanked us profusely, praising Allah. Then they urged us, "Come", and we went down to the village together, with them insisting on carrying our backpacks. The first place we visited was the mosque. We met the *imam*, who was very nice, and told him we had come with Injils. He said that was very good.

"We have only one Quran in the village," he explained, "and I've always wanted to read the Torah and the Zabur and Injil."

We had two special Arabic editions among the books that we carried. I took one out and gave it to him.

"Oh!" He touched the Scriptures with awe. "For so many years I've wanted to read this."

We were then taken to the head man of the village, and presented him with a copy too. He was absolutely thrilled, and shouted to the other men to bring carpets. Rattan mats were hastily laid down over the dirt in the square, and women came to serve little glasses of sweet tea and other refreshments.

My companion whispered, "Tom, I don't know any Arabic."

"Neither do I," I admitted.

"But you know some words?"

"Only a few – mostly just greetings."

"Then what are we going to do?" he asked me, frustrated. "How can we share the gospel with these people?"

"That's up to God."

Already the people were poring over the Scriptures with wonder. They pointed to verses and began to ask, "What does this mean?" and "What about this?"

It was wonderful to see their fascination with God's Word. Then a thirteen-year-old boy came over to introduce himself.

"I am the only boy in the village who can read and speak English," he said proudly, and then offered, "Can I interpret for you?"

Wow, I thought. God provided.

We spent the next couple of hours unfolding God's good news to the villagers through this young boy. He was so eager, so excited. But then, suddenly, our visit came to an abrupt halt as I felt something sting my foot through the rattan mat we were sitting on.

The pain of a scorpion bite is indescribable. My foot began immediately to swell, and as soon as the villagers learned what had happened they tried to help, hurrying to apply some kind of home-made remedy to the sting. Then the men lifted me and carried me back up the mountain and down to where we left the four-wheel drive, so I could be taken to hospital. A scorpion bite can cause an array of severe symptoms including seizures, blurred vision, and difficulty breathing – sometimes even death.

I was already very ill. The boy who had been translating for us had followed us to the car. He came up to the window to speak to me.

"Sir," he implored, his anxiety that others have an opportunity to hear the good news overcoming even his concern for me, "what about the other villages?" They too had listened to the radio broadcasts (Feba's Love and Faithfulness programme), he said, but they had no Scriptures in Arabic.

I explained to the boy that I was very sorry that I was unable to take the books to any other villages, as I needed to get medical treatment urgently.

He didn't hesitate. "Can I take them please?" he pleaded.

The last glimpse I had of this youth he was setting off towards another mountain, with the knapsack of Scriptures on his back. I have prayed many times that the Lord used him to fulfil His purposes in that remote, mountainous area of Arabia.

* * *

Of course, as I explained earlier, my most common method for distributing God's Word in city thoroughfares and hotels was simply carrying transparent shopping bags full of Bibles and New Testaments. I was walking along the street in Bahrain one day when a man who was probably in his forties came running after me.

"Mr Thomas, Mr Thomas!" he panted, obviously out of breath.

"Take it easy," I urged. "Get your breath back." So the man waited a moment and smiled at me.

"Mr Thomas, I am a Christian because of you and your courage," he announced.

Of course I was delighted to hear such a bold confession of faith from anyone in this small Muslim kingdom, and asked the man to tell me his story.

"Two and a half years ago you gave me a Bible in Qatar and spoke to me about it being the true Word of God," he told me earnestly. "Through reading it I came to faith in Jesus Christ as my Saviour. I left Islam and am now a member of a Christian church."

A single seed, sown randomly, had taken root.

Although we rarely got to hear such stories directly from individuals, the transforming power of a single Bible was continually brought home to us. In Cyprus we received a letter from another former Muslim:

> Since I received the Bible in my own language which you sent, I have shared it with my family and many friends, and have found that our Saviour is Jesus Christ,

the only way to God. The Bible is an inspiring fountain of life to me. Other friends, including my own brother, desire personal copies. Can you kindly send more?

Edna and I remember the occasion that we stayed overnight in a hotel in Sharjah, United Arab Emirates, because accommodation was offered free with our air tickets. We went into the hotel restaurant for a meal and were seated by the manager in charge. After studying my face intently, he smiled and said, "Do you remember me, sir?"

"I'm sorry, I can't say I do," I confessed. "Please don't be offended."

"I am not offended at all. But I am sure you are the man who gave me a Bible at a petrol station in Oman. You had a friend with you. I am now a committed Christian through reading that Bible."

Of course Edna and I were thrilled to hear the man's declaration. He sent one of his staff to his private room with his keys, instructing him to bring down the Bible beside his bed. The fellow complied and the manager reverently handed me the Book.

"Here it is," he said, "the Bible you gave me. It is so precious to me. God speaks to me through it every day and shows me wonderful insights."

We opened it and found the pages full of underlined verses along with handwritten notes beside various passages and promises. We embraced each other then as brothers, and he told me, "I am indebted to you for speaking to me at that petrol station in the interior of Oman, and giving me the Word of God."

The promise of Ecclesiastes 11:1 came to me: "Ship

your grain across the sea; after many days you may receive a return."

We will have to wait until heaven to feast on the thousands of other stories of God's amazing grace.

6
FOLLOWING GOD'S GPS

In a Bahrain airport I once ran into a local man who asked if I was from England.

"I have a fifteenth-century manor house in the UK," he announced proudly. "I have taken one wife and four children there."

"So why are you here in Bahrain?" I asked.

"I'm visiting my other wife. We have another five children. I hope to take them to England too someday."

"Oh. Are you going back to England now?"

"No, I'm going to Thailand."

"A business trip?"

"No, I'm going to play with the girls," the man smirked.

I've always found that on each occasion you are confronted with, the Holy Spirit will direct you as to what you should say or do at the time. My response came immediately and without hesitation.

"AIDS is spreading all over the world, and you are going to see prostitutes and take AIDS back to your wives and children? God will judge you."

He ran out of that men's room with fear written on his face. When I emerged he was talking to another man, and pointed at me. It must have been a security agent. Obviously he wanted to have me arrested, but the official refused.

During my many visits to Gulf states I have also encountered people of great integrity, both nationals and minority workers. Yet it is an unhappy fact that many guest workers in this part of the world suffer harsh treatment. Sometimes their salaries are held back by their Arab employers and they are robbed of what is their due. There are also shocking reports of abuse to Filipina women who are employed as maids or nursemaids. Some of these ladies are Christians who have served as emissaries of Christ, introducing their small charges to Jesus. Dozens of large, fervent congregations of Filipinos and other nationalities thrive in the larger Gulf cities.

One Filipino brother told me about a fellow believer who had visited a government hospital to see a non-Christian friend who was dying of cancer. The man was in a ward with three other cancer patients. One was an Arab from Saudi Arabia.

The Filipino sat beside his friend and opened his New Testament to read aloud the passage about the woman who had suffered for twelve years with an issue of blood. When she heard that Jesus was passing by she pushed through the crowds and managed to touch the hem of His clothing. Instantly she felt herself healed. He encouraged his friend to reach out to Jesus for salvation and healing, but the latter resisted.

"Please, let me pray for you before I leave," he finally said. He prayed with passion, but to his surprise and sadness the man continued to refuse to trust the Lord. As he stood up and prepared to leave the ward, the Arab man in the other bed suddenly called out.

"I want you to pray for me, please. I heard what you said about Isa (Jesus) and the woman."

So the Christian went to this man's bedside, shared further about Jesus, then prayed for him. They shook hands and the believer left.

A few days later the Filipino went back to the hospital to urge his friend once more to call upon the Lord. But he had already passed away, and the bed which the Arab patient had occupied was also empty.

As he was leaving the ward a male nurse spoke up and said the Saudi man had left him a note. He handed it over. The message expressed warm thanks, and explained that the surgeon had found no more cancer in his body. He was returning home to tell all of his family that it was Isa who had forgiven his sins and healed him. "From now on," he added, "all my prayers will be in His name."

A close friend of mine was approached by a Muslim who started to argue forcibly that Allah was the only God. My friend said, "Stop, please. Wait. Before we talk further together I want to pray."

The Arab was surprised but agreed. He listened quietly as my friend prayed. After he finished he said, "Now you can ask your questions."

The man replied, "I do not have any more questions. As you prayed I felt the holy presence of God for the first time in my life."

My friend shared the gospel message with the Arab and he gladly accepted a copy of the New Testament.

* * *

My first visit to Syria in 1988–89 left a deep impression on me. I travelled to Homs, the third largest city after Damascus and Aleppo and which boasted a substantial minority of

Christians and Alawites[4] besides Muslims. In fact, between 6 and 10 per cent of Syria's population (1.5 million, including Christian refugees from Iraq) were non-Muslims. The Christian community had been tolerated for centuries in this country, and had enjoyed peace and religious freedom under the Assad regime. There were a number of churches.

For several days I had the privilege of meeting with true believers in Jesus Christ. Some of them had come out of Islam and others were brought up in Christian families, but the unity among them was precious to see, although the secret police sometimes threatened them. I have often since then remembered those brothers and sisters in Christ with great affection, even more so now that the city, including its churches, has been destroyed by the evil activity of ISIS. Altogether more than nine million Syrians have been displaced, over four million of them fleeing as refugees to neighbouring countries.[5]

On that trip my travels took me to another city, where I was asked to preach the Word to a congregation of about forty believers. I gladly accepted the opportunity. A pastor led the service and one could sense the love of Jesus abounding and overflowing these peoples' hearts. I could not help wishing the same exuberance was as present in some of our staid and stuffy services in the West, which are so often dominated by formalism and ritualism. Instead of reading prayers, these

---

4 Alawites represent about 12 per cent of the Syrian population. Although they are an offshoot of Shia Islam they are often looked down upon because of secret, syncretistic beliefs like reincarnation. Followers may even bear Christian names and celebrate Christmas as well as a special, male-only mass (some Alawites don't believe women have souls or don't reincarnate). The shrines of tombs are their only structures of worship.

5 Figures are accurate at the time of writing according to the UN High Commissioner for Refugees (UNHCR).

believers prayed and worshipped extemporaneously from their hearts. When it was time for me to preach I stood up with my Bible and opened it. The pastor, who was translating for me, whispered into my ear, "Those three men who just came are secret police. Be careful."

I looked up and smiled at the men as they sat down in the back. Quickly sending up a silent prayer, I felt the Lord directing me to read from 2 Corinthians chapter 5, verses 11 to 21, about God's love compelling us to serve as His ambassadors. I then began my message by observing how it's a common belief that all English people are Christians because they are "born Christian". I wanted to emphasize that no one can be born a Christian because we are all born in sin, into a sinful world.

Under the Holy Spirit's anointing I went on to share my own life story and how I was "born again", born into God's family and transformed into an entirely new creation in Jesus. I cannot remember how long I spoke, but no one moved until I closed the service in prayer.

The three men immediately came to the front, smiling, to shake my hand and thank me for what I had shared. They were Muslims but truly interested, and asked me further questions. I offered them individual Gospels in Arabic and they accepted them willingly. They wanted to know if I was going to speak again the following week, but I said I would be leaving the country and returning to Cyprus. The pastor and congregation rejoiced, for these men were usually surly and asked for money. On this occasion they did not.

I was only able to visit in the north of Syria again years later, in 1996. On that occasion I met with a group of dedicated Christian Syrians who were reaching out to

Muslims. A decision was made at that time to establish a Christian bookshop, with an extra room for counselling enquirers. Although I tried to go to this country again from Cyprus, I was refused a visa, with no reason given. However, the bookshop did open, and national workers were encouraged to see the increased desire of Muslims for the Word of God.

We all know about the horrors visited upon this country since the outbreak of civil war in 2011 and the atrocities committed by ISIS. Several hundred thousand people have been killed – half of them civilians – and millions have been uprooted from their homes. Believers worldwide need to partner in asking God to keep Syria from becoming another country suffocated by extremist Islam and Sharia law.

Lord Jesus, only you know which of your followers in Syria still live on this earth. Those who do not are with you, robed in righteousness and enjoying the peace and pleasure of your kingdom.

Lord, have mercy. Set your people free!

* * *

In 2011 the country of Sudan officially divided into two countries, with South Sudan becoming independent. Christians celebrated, for in the years leading up to this the government and National Islamic Front had practised a *jihad* (holy war) which made life intolerable for the non-Muslim minority. Military oppression, bombings, terrorism, and religious-oriented murders (martyrdoms) were common: so was the rape and abduction of women, restrictions on travel, and roadblocks. Over a million people were killed during this unholy religious civil war… More than a million more were displaced from their homes, forced to live in refugee camps or beg on the streets. The country had one of the world's lowest life expectancies and highest infant mortality rates.

Nothing in all of our travels compared with the appalling suffering of Sudanese Christians I saw on my visit in 1997. One refugee camp alone contained over four thousand children – mostly orphans – who lived on a single meal a day consisting of rice or maize with occasional traces of meat or vegetables. As a result these children were chronically malnourished and vulnerable to disease. I was horrified to learn that some Islamic relief authorities told them they could have all the food and water they wanted, plus a proper education, if they would change their names to Muslim names. Not one child in that camp agreed to change their name.

On the other hand I was moved and humbled to see the love of our OM team members, along with over seventy Christian Sudanese volunteers who were themselves displaced and who had lost everything, helping the children in these camps. Some men and women were trained teachers who gave the children schooling, taught them Scriptures, sang with them, and fed them meals.

Back in Cyprus, Edna and I spread the news and sent out urgent appeals to assist the creation of an income-generating chicken farm project, plus an accommodation block for some of the workers. Barnabas Fund in the UK came through with a large gift, and individuals and fellowships responded from Australia, the Gulf, Singapore, and the UK.

The total donation of over US$50,000 not only covered

the farm and housing projects, but provided an urgently needed land cruiser, second-hand but in good condition, as well as donkeys to fetch water from the Nile River, about 10 miles from refugee camps. Other funds bought goats to furnish families with milk, cheese, and yogurt; plus grinding mills and tools for general maintenance that would help support OMers and volunteers.

During my visit to Sudan I spent time with the OM team's ten-day book exhibition in the centre of Khartoum. These exhibitions were a major ministry for a number of years and had proven remarkably popular. This time the event drew almost six thousand visitors, about two-thirds of them Muslims. Arabic Bibles were sold at the subsidized rate of just over two US dollars and New Testaments for one dollar. Over six hundred Bibles and a thousand New Testaments were purchased, as well as many children's coloured Bible story books. Every visitor also received the free gift of an Arabic Gospel of John or Luke. In a separate tent we screened continuous showings of the *Jesus* film. Many Muslim university students came day after day to ask serious questions.

Two particular incidents thrilled us. A former fundamentalist came into the large exhibition tent to ask the team's forgiveness for his past hatred and actions against Christians. The team members gladly embraced the man and prayed for him. Although he was still a Muslim he accepted the gift of an Arabic Bible.

The second incident involved a fine-looking gentleman who turned out to be an Islamic scholar. After looking over the books in the exhibition he spent US$150 on Bibles plus a Bible dictionary, concordance, and commentary. When he paid for them he smiled and told the person helping him, "I am seeking truth."

Down in the southern city of Malakal, a team of eight put on a book exhibition during the days and meetings each night. A number of Muslims from a mosque stirred up opposition and attacked the team, accusing them of insulting Islam. Police arrested the eight and put them in prison "for their protection".

For two days the OMers sang, prayed, and preached in their prison cell. Nominal Christians in the city rose up to protest their imprisonment and went to see the governor. If the team was not released within twenty-four hours, they warned him, things could get ugly.

Shortly afterwards the governor had the team members released and gave them permission to use the local youth sports hall for their exhibition and meetings. I understand that over a hundred people turned to the Lord as a result, some of them university students and a good number of them Muslims.

Christians were commonly imprisoned. I heard of one outstandingly bold Sudanese believer who was arrested on false charges and beaten. One day his interrogators made him stand and face a wall for five hours, all the time demanding that he recite the shahada or Muslim creed in Arabic: "There is no god but Allah, and Muhammad is his messenger."

The Christian remained silent. They beat him again, and after a while came back to threaten him with death. This time he replied, "You should not disturb me when I am praying."

Amazingly, his captors apologized but added, "You may

pray for thirty minutes only, then you will have another beating." The follower of Christ began to pray anointed prayers in a loud voice. The thirty minutes elapsed and he waited for the further beating, but there was silence. Hearts had been moved and even melted. The prison officers apologized, and the man was released.

The Republic of Sudan has seen big changes in recent years. Omar al-Bashir's military government introduced Islamic law on a national level, forcing most Christians to flee to South Sudan. Permission for a book exhibition like the one described above would certainly not be granted in Khartoum these days; authorities are suppressing all manifestations of Christianity and putting enormous pressure on non-Muslims to either convert or leave.

One big consignment of Bibles we sent to North Sudan was confiscated and sent to a factory for shredding. The shredding machine started up, but before a single copy went through the equipment broke down. An experienced technician was just starting to look for the cause when the motor suddenly started up again and he lost one arm. Such shock and fear came upon the workers that no one wanted to shred the Bibles or destroy them by fire. They were sure it was God's judgment for attempting to destroy His Word. They chose to give them back to the Christians who had brought them into the country.

Since the division of Sudan some OMers have spent time in prison and been expelled. A team continues to minister to the needy in South Sudan, however, despite personal danger and the new nation's inadequate infrastructure. World Christians need to intercede for their protection against disease and violence between tribes.

* * *

We made several visits to Bulgaria, the first one in 1990 to spy out the land. Edna and I were actually en route to London, but knowing we were to have a thirty-six-hour stopover in Sofia, we had carried several strong suitcases packed with Bulgarian language Bibles and New Testaments. We had discovered these in the Cyprus Bible Society store. Since they had been there for a long time and the staff were glad to see this material being used, we were able to purchase it at a very reasonable price.

After arriving at Sofia International Airport we approached customs with two trolleys. A large-sized customs officer looked us over and asked, "What currency do you have on you?" I jumped to the wrong conclusion that he wanted a bribe, and prepared myself.

I opened my wallet and showed him American dollars and English pounds. He looked closely at the bills and then enquired, "Do you intend to change some dollars into our currency – the *lev* – to spend while you are here?"

"Of course we do," I responded.

"Good. Go through."

We smiled and thanked the man and proceeded through customs. Not a single case was opened for inspection. We were elated.

During our taxi ride to the hotel we made friends with the driver and gave him a Bible.

"I cannot afford to pay for this," he told us.

We assured him it was a gift and added a tip when we paid for the taxi ride. At the hotel several staff helped us with our heavy cases. Before they left our room we opened one and their eyes nearly popped out of their heads. We offered each person a Bible which they accepted with joy, hugging us.

Edna and I started settling into the room, feeling a little tired, but people kept knocking on the door, again and again, as staff came from all over the hotel to ask if they too could have a Bible. We were thrilled to comply, of course, and even had prayer with some of them. They in turn presented us with a bouquet of lovely fresh flowers.

Edna woke earlier than I did the next morning and called me to the window. "Oh, Tom! See this. See this!"

It was bitterly cold outside. Together we watched as a queue of people at least a quarter of a mile long, two and three deep, waited for their daily allowance of a loaf of bread. Pensioners who had lived most of their lives under Communism were granted a weekly allowance that allowed them to buy two loaves of bread and a gallon of kerosene. One pain relief tablet would cost half their pension. Hospitals were without sheets, bandages, medicines, food or blood banks. Inflation was at 300 per cent for six months and the average men's wage was $10 or $20 per month. The scene below humbled us and we prayed to our Abba Father, giving thanks that we were able to bring His living bread into Sofia even though these dear people also needed bread for their stomachs to survive.

We didn't feel much like consuming breakfast after that but we did have a pot of tea to fortify ourselves against the cold. We decided to take Bibles around the city in strong plastic bags and sow our "living bread". Many people smiled and kissed the Bibles as we offered them. Not one refused.

When we saw a big Bulgarian Orthodox church we went inside. A number of people were there, playing beautiful music on violins and other instruments. Every wall was decorated with marvellous biblical murals, although they needed cleaning because they had been darkened by years of burning candles and incense.

We had only a few Bulgarian Bibles left but at that moment we spotted a very old lady, poorly dressed with sackcloth tied around her legs for warmth. She was sitting on some steps, listening to the music, and when we approached to offer her a Bible I will never forget her response. She reverently took the Book in her hands and kissed it several times, with tears running down her cheeks. We could not speak Bulgarian and she could not speak English, but as we hugged one another the words of an old hymn came to mind: "Blessed be the tie that binds our hearts in Christian love."

OMer Ray Amey joined me on my next visit to Bulgaria, in the winter of 1991. Ray was earnestly keen on spreading literature, not only Bibles but all kinds of Christian material, particularly in the Middle East. We had been impressed by his attractive displays using a variety of excellent resources.

Our aim on this trip was to do personal distribution of Bulgarian Bibles and New Testaments on the streets of Sofia and Plovdiv. But oh, how cold it was! Deep snow was everywhere and we could never seem to keep warm. Yet although the weather seemed against us the people were for us.

We went into the same Orthodox church that Edna and I had entered on our previous trip. No music this time but there were plenty of people. The interior was still very cold, but all the burning candles acted as the church's central heating. As we mingled with people and sowed God's Word among them, I noticed one young lady sitting in a pew near the wall. The light from outside was bright with the snow's reflection and seemed to bathe her. The girl was leaning over, reading from a small book, so Ray and I made our way over to her.

"What are you reading?" I asked, wondering if she knew any English. Her face lit up and she lifted the little book higher for us to see.

"I am reading a Gideon's New Testament!"

We were taken by surprise, but delighted. I then raised a copy of the Bulgarian Bible in my hand.

"But do you have one of these to read?"

She gave a loud exclamation of joy. "Oh! The whole, complete Bible! We have been praying to the Lord for Bibles in Bulgarian. Allelujah!"

The girl, whose name was Tanya, went on to tell us that there was a small but growing number of university students who had been "born again". Since they had no Bibles they all shared her Gideon's New Testament.

"We have a meeting tonight in the flat of an elderly lady. Could you join us, and share your testimony and teaching?"

We eagerly agreed.

Ray and I loaded up with Bibles and accompanied Tanya to the lady's apartment. She spoke no English but welcomed us gladly, and so did the young students who piled in. What an evening! The presence of the Lord was in our midst, and some of those young people actually wept when they received their own copies of the Bible.

We shared our testimonies, but felt humbled as we listened to theirs. Some of their parents had suffered under their country's repressive regime; some had also died too young. The next generation had begun to hunger for the truth that could set them free. Thankfully, it wasn't someone from a false sect that came to them. Some Americans visited Bulgaria on a US government trade mission and one of their number was on a higher mission: to sow the truth of the gospel. This man had brought Gideon New Testaments in his luggage, and in the evenings he walked around the city offering them to people who could read English. Tanya was one of those people, and that encounter had brought her to the end of her search – to Jesus, the light of the world.

That was the highlight of our visit. Freezing cold on the outside but holy fire within; joy unspeakable and full of glory! I was so happy I felt like I could have carried Ray piggyback all the way back to the hotel, though he was no featherweight. For the next three or more years after that, we sent 10-kilo parcels of Bulgarian Bibles from Cyprus to Tanya and her group, at regular intervals.

Once God enabled me to get a few thousand Bibles from the United Bible Society in Stuttgart, Germany, and send them to a growing ministry in Sofia, Plovdiv, and other areas of the country. Another time, on the way back to Cyprus from the UK after some speaking engagements, I was able to take 60 kilos of food and medicine to very needy Christians in Plovdiv.

Following God's global heart was an endless adventure.

7
YEMEN: CHRIST AT WORK IN THE CRADLE OF ISLAM

E ven though it has been around for four thousand years, many people would have trouble pinpointing Yemen on a map of the world. The legendary land of the Queen of Sheba lies below Saudi Arabia and occupies the southwest corner of the Arabian Peninsula. For scenery it's hard to beat with majestic mountains, a stunning coastline along the Red and Arabian Seas, even desert sand dunes complete with camels. The architecture of the old cities is uniquely beautiful, and in their colourful market *souqs* you can still buy frankincense and myrrh.

There's not much gold to be had, however. Yemen is the poorest country in the Arab world, with half of its 26 million people in need of some kind of humanitarian help. In spite of this, women average seven children each and many families have ten to fifteen. Almost half the population is under the age of fifteen. Females have a particularly hard time of it. The country has the lowest school enrolment of girls in the Middle East, leaving over half of females illiterate.

Yemen is also the cradle of Islam; 99.9 per cent of residents consider themselves guardians of the faith, although many cannot read the Quran for themselves and only repeat what they are taught. This is Osama bin Laden's ancestral homeland and where he and Saddam Hussein are still considered heroes.

The southern part of the country was a British Protectorate for a hundred and forty years. An uprising that resulted in the deaths of many British finally led to independence in 1967. The Russians who were then invited in helped themselves to a lot of the property that was left behind.

Towards the end of 1992, Anglican bishop John Brown asked if Edna and I could be seconded from OM for three months, in order to start the restoration of Christ Church in Aden. Twenty-two churches of many denominations had once held services in that city. Now they were all gone, but the Grand Mufti of Yemen had given permission to restore one place of worship. Christ Church was the logical choice. The largest and oldest building, it had originally been created in 1863 as the garrison church for British forces, with Queen Victoria herself giving one hundred gold sovereigns for the purpose. As an eighteen-year-old soldier I had landed in Aden in 1955 and worshipped in this very church. I never imagined that God would bring me back one day to restore it!

I had assured Edna that it was a beautiful building. When we got there in January 1993, however, we were confronted with a total wreck. Graffiti covered the walls that remained and rubbish of all kinds, including human excrement, had been strewn everywhere as it had in other places of Christian worship, in a deliberate act of desecration. We had no place to stay and no money, but a Canadian oil company in Aden kindly lent us a flat in the city for a month, until we could find something else.

I was probably the only Westerner in Yemen who wasn't driving around in an air-conditioned vehicle. I managed to buy an old bike very cheaply and after being knocked off twice by careless drivers on the pothole-ridden roads, I went to the oil company and asked if they could spare a hard helmet. They gave me a bright white one. A couple of days later I felt prompted to paint across it: "Trinity Company". Whenever I was stopped at company gates or at hospitals, shops or government offices men would ask me where Trinity Company was, because they were looking for employment. I told them the offices were in the tallest building of the world and there were three main directors who always agreed with each other. They were in unity because they were trinity.

This provoked some great conversations. People quickly picked up on what I was really saying, so when I produced free Injils for them they were delighted. Not once on those occasions did I have problems. In fact, a number asked me if I had heard of a certain very good Christian radio programme in Arabic. They knew the names of the producers and of the question and answer programmes, and spoke highly of them. Some men even caught my eye and made the sign of the cross over their hearts. Thank God for the ministry of these programmes!

I became known as the Injil man. In every shop I would lay a copy down on the counter and people would ask what it was and how much money it would cost them. I said it was free, but only for those who wanted to know the truth about Isa. Within twelve days I gave away 4,800 copies.

In spite of having the Grand Mufti's okay to rebuild Christ Church we had no deed to prove ownership. That led to a long, dusty search through government archives. The deeds to twenty-one other churches in Yemen were found, but not Christ Church. Authorities obviously wanted money under the table and people asked why I didn't pay them. I responded, should we use the money people gave us for this project to pay bribes?

So we asked people to fast and pray for a miracle, and this is how it happened. A Muslim friend named Mustafa felt so bad about the way I was being treated by various government departments he decided to go to the office himself to ask them to search again for the deeds. He came away feeling very discouraged.

At the bottom of the steps to the government building he saw a blind man begging. He put some money into the man's hands, and was asked why he was there. Mustafa explained.

The man told him, "Before I became blind I worked in this office. I know where those deeds are."

Mustafa took the man back into the office, and the man directed the staff where to look. They pulled a great old dusty register off the shelf. The termites had been at it and it was full of fragments. But there, in indelible ink, was the land grant number of the church, for the vicarage, the Sunday School hall, and Christ Church, with the date.

To think God used two Muslims to find the deeds! I went back to the right office with photocopies and we got the property.

The next step was to find a contractor. An Englishman we met wanted US$100,000 to do the work with a $10,000 deposit up front. I told him we had no funds but we had a great God. The man wasn't impressed. He was an atheist and used some strong language, but we eventually became the best of friends.

The work on the desecrated church began with a flourish. The contractor soon had his workers on the site, clearing the refuse inside the building, which was knee deep. It was awful, stinking filth: piles of human excreta filling both vestries and parts of the chancel. They took two days to remove it all, but seeing it completely cleaned up was a real tonic to Edna and me, reminding us of Hezekiah and the clean-up job he ordered on the house of God in his time. Then the workmen went up on the roof, repairing and replacing the scores of missing and broken tiles. Others dug deep to see if there was serious damage to the foundations. We were impressed by those labourers. They were truly workers, not shirkers.

Then came the day we commenced the reconstruction of an 8-foot-high wall that was to surround the church compound, which was the culturally expected thing. I was doing some work in the house we had found to rent, which was also used for prayer meetings and Bible studies throughout the week. The phone rang. John, the contractor, was definitely not his usual calm and collected self.

"Tom," he exclaimed tensely, "You'd better get down to the church site ASAP."

"Is anything wrong?" I asked.

"*Wrong?* I'll say something's wrong! There are soldiers and other men all over the site with guns, telling us to get off the land because it doesn't belong to us. They say it belongs to the naval commander, and the old church building is a storeroom for naval equipment!"

John went on to say that the intruders had brought all kinds of material onto the site, including cement mixers, bags of sand, and cement and breeze blocks, and were going to build on the church land. His work force was petrified, so he had withdrawn over thirty men and told them to go home.

"All right, John. I'll go down and meet these people and try to sort it out, God helping me."

His reply didn't reflect confidence in this strategy. However, I immediately got on my trusty bicycle and pedalled to the church site. John had certainly given me a clear picture of the situation. The place was crawling with military and workmen, both inside and outside the church building.

"Who's in charge here?" I shouted. I had to repeat this question several times before a menacing-looking group gathered around me.

"This Christian church was built in 1863 with Queen Victoria's approval. It is now the property of Her Majesty Queen Elizabeth in England, who is head of the Anglican Church worldwide. And I am her representative," I added, pointing a finger at my chest. I regret that I hadn't had the chance to ask my queen for her permission.

A stunned silence greeted these words. I was praying under my breath, "Lord, it is time for you to work!"

Then the crowd began to murmur. The guns that had been pointing at me were lowered. And before my very eyes the men began to withdraw. Workers were directed to load the breeze blocks onto a lorry. Cement mixers and bags of sand and cement were also removed, and off they all went in a cloud of dust. Within a short time I stood alone on the property, bursting with wonder and joy at the power of my Abba Father, Jesus His Son my Saviour, and the Holy Spirit. Shouting, "Praise be to Isa (Jesus)!" I went to find John and tell him what had happened. He seemed subdued by the news and I knew that he too was awestruck by the unexpected outcome.

"John," I said, "I think we must get the wall up as quickly as we possibly can." He agreed, and his men succeeded in building a fine wall indeed.

It wasn't long before my contractor called me into his office to state that he'd already used $10,000 and needed a further $10,000 – *at once*! I opened my briefcase and handed him a cheque for the required amount.

"This arrived yesterday," I told him. He stared at me in disbelief and I grinned. "That's the God I serve!"

John returned my smile. A few years later when another man took over responsibility for the building, an ordained priest, he told the contractor that he had little money to pay a bill. This atheist contractor responded, "You had better talk to the same God that Tom and Edna Hamblin talked to. He always answered them!"

Eventually we were to see the church rebuilt, along with the creation of several lovely, air-conditioned, en suite bedrooms and a large lounge upstairs, plus a fully equipped kitchen and dining area downstairs. In addition there was a large area for social events and an office. The main worship area on the ground floor could accommodate up to a hundred and fifty persons.

We also gradually added two clinics within the compound, one to treat general medical conditions and the other an eye clinic, along with medical staff accommodation. "River blindness" caused by parasites is just one of many eye diseases that commonly plague residents of developing nations like Yemen. Both clinics served free of charge and were kept very busy from the day they opened. At first patients came in their hundreds, but mercifully for all the staff concerned, the numbers reduced over time to more manageable quantities. Nursing staff volunteered from the UK, Netherlands, Germany, Australia, and Singapore. All were very dedicated. We also had short-term volunteers who worked hard; there were no drones in this busy beehive!

Many of the patients came to me to ask for the holy Injil. They were overjoyed to receive it, and went away hiding it in their robes.

Some time after we were established the watchman at the gate came to report that there was a group of people wanting to go inside the sanctuary.

"Let them go in, then," I responded.

"But they're mountain people!" His expression conveyed his disapproval of allowing such a lowly rabble inside the sacred precincts.

"If they have come all this way and want to see the church, let them come!"

I welcomed a large, humbly dressed group that included women and children, and led them into the sanctuary. As soon as the people spotted the table at the front that held a wooden cross, tears of joy began to overflow and run down their faces.

"Isa! Oh, Isa!" they cried emotionally and told me, "We love Jesus." They explained that they were believers, and had heard on a Christian radio broadcast that there was a church in their land.

They kept repeating the word "water", using hand motions. I had already given them bottles of drinking water, so it took a few moments before it finally dawned on me why these villagers had made the long trek from the mountains.

They wanted to be baptized.

At this time in Yemen the baptism of believers could only take place secretly, in the sea. If we had openly performed the ceremony I would have been deported and the church closed. I explained that the Bible allowed for believers to be baptized anywhere, even at home. It did not have to take place in a church.

I gave a short demonstration by taking an empty bucket and overturning it over the leader's head. I explained in simple English that they could baptize each other in God's name. Their eyes lit up with relief and they hugged me, kissing me on both cheeks in the traditional manner.

When I asked if they knew of any others in the mountains who believed in Jesus, their answer thrilled me. "There are many, many who love Isa," they assured me, "even though we cannot get Injils to read His Word." I learned that in one small village alone there were seventy-eight believers. The women gladly accepted quantities of New Testaments to take back, which they hid underneath their robes. We gave them more cold drinks and refreshments before they set out on their three-day walk home.

A Muslim man who was also from the mountains came to listen to me explain the truth for several weeks. He then asked for a Bible. As I always did when this happened, I put my hands on Ferez and prayed that he would receive a full revelation of God's Word through reading it. Then I carefully wrapped the Bible and placed it in a bag so that nobody could see what he was carrying.

When Ferez left Aden and returned home he shared his newfound faith with his wife and sons, and they too put their trust in Jesus. They became a secret family of believers. However, news of the man's conversion got out, and someone came to warn him that the religious police were looking for him. He was forced to flee, not telling his wife where he was going so that she could truthfully tell the police she didn't know.

Ferez left his wife and one son in the house; the other son was on the other side of the mountain, looking after sheep. This boy had taken his father's Arabic Bible with him and he was reading it when the *mutawa* found him. They killed him and laid his dead body at the feet of Ferez's wife.

"Tell Ferez this is what will happen to him and to all of you unless you return to Islam."

Ferez left the country and eventually ended up in Bangkok. People who were in trouble could generally get into Thailand at that time without difficulties. He went looking for a church and found a fine evangelical fellowship in the city. One of the people he met was a missionary from Holland who took Ferez in and mentored him in his new faith. This man also started the process of trying to get him into a free country along with his wife and son.

By "chance" a Christian lady in Ireland received an email message, asking if anyone knew a Tom Hamblin who had lived in Yemen. She called me, and as a result I made contact with the missionary. He told me that Ferez was doing well, but that he could no longer stay in Thailand because enemies had learned where he was. He needed to be moved to a place of safety.

We wrote letters to various governments to present the case. Canada agreed at first to take Ferez and his family but then changed its mind. The glad news is that Ferez flew to the Netherlands instead, where the missionary was on furlough, and that country accepted him. Ferez took the Christian name of David, and after several years he was eventually reunited with his wife and son.

The three months Edna and I had intended to stay in Yemen stretched to almost four years, on and off, by the time we finished our work there. But in May 1994, the unification agreement of North and South dissolved under the North's corrupt and heavy-handed rule. The country exploded into civil war.

Just the week before, my cardiologist had advised me that I could stay in Aden until July, when we planned to take a month's break in England before completing the project. "But," he cautioned me, "don't get into stressful situations!"

On the first night of bombing we stood in our garden and watched the Northern air force planes pass overhead and drop their deadly load on Aden airport. We lived only three minutes away. Huge clouds of smoke went up as the terminal building and several hangars were destroyed, taking the lives of a number of local people.

Our construction of Christ Church and other buildings on the compound was by this time about 60 per cent complete. I had been scheduled to speak at the family service two days after the invasion, and had chosen Romans 8:28 as my text: "And we know that in all things God works for the good of those who love him, who have been called according to his purpose."

We had cause to think of that verse during the next harrowing days, as all expats were evacuated from Yemen. The oil company homes were all damaged and pillaged, as well as their beautiful clinic. The company was marvellous to Edna and me, treating us as if we were their employees.

They arranged to transport us to the port along with everyone else. While about six hundred people of every nationality waited on the quayside for landing craft to take us to a French warship, anchored some distance offshore, children who belonged to our church's "King's Club" started to sing choruses.

"Come on Uncle Tom, Auntie Edna!" they shouted. "Tell us some Bible stories!" We obliged and even threw in a Bible quiz, with a great audience listening intently. At one point a North Yemen fighter plane swooped overhead to bomb the port and we all dived for cover. Thankfully no one was injured and we were all eventually conveyed to the French rescue vessel. Over the next three days many of the passengers came to confide to Edna and me that their fears had been calmed by the songs and prayers. God's presence was real and as always He was working "all things for good".

Because none of us were allowed to carry more than 10 kilos of our personal possessions, everything else we owned was left behind. When the ship reached Djibouti, on the Horn of Africa, the company gave us seats at no cost on a charter flight to England. At Stanstead Airport we were included in a night's stopover at the Hilton Hotel. This gave us a chance to make calls, shower, and sleep before we parted from our many friends and made our way back to Cyprus on another flight.

Arriving back on the island at 3:30 in the morning. Edna sailed through immigration without a hitch. The officer on duty stopped me, however, and advised, "There is a problem. Follow me."

Ushered into the Chief Immigration Officer's office, I was stunned when this gentleman looked at me grimly and announced, "There is a warrant out for your arrest!"

This isn't the Arabian Gulf or Saudi, I reminded myself, bewildered. *They must have the wrong man!*

The mystery was eventually solved by a traffic police officer. Over a year before I had been involved in a minor road accident, but I couldn't attend the court hearing six months later because I was in Yemen. I had written letters to the police and justice department and Edna had spoken to them personally to explain the reason for my non-appearance. They had assured her it was no problem; I could straighten it out when I got back to Cyprus. So the whole thing was blamed on a computer error and I was released after paying a £25 fine.

Edna and I took a break during July and August, allowing ourselves to take an in-depth look at our priorities. I also had a medical check-up. The results of an angiogram were positive: no blockage in my main arteries. But the doctor strongly advised me to slow down or else change my lifestyle.

After consulting with leaders of our church in Reading and OM, we came to the consensus that I should curtail the constant travelling to Gulf countries and carrying heavy consignments of Scriptures as excess cabin baggage. However, we would still act as conduits, receiving shipments and providing God's Word to sowers in each country. We would also continue to visit and encourage His people in Muslim hotspots.

8
YEMEN: STARTING OVER

I returned to Aden in September, two months after the end of the civil war. Because the country was still regarded as unsafe, Edna stayed behind until the end of the month, when I found a villa we could live in.

We both wept at the devastation. Our contractors had left security men to watch over the property but once again, Christ Church was in ruins. Rebel mobs had even taken doors and beams, stripped the wiring from the walls, stolen the wash basins, and cleaned out a container holding all the large, new tiles just delivered to cover the church's floor. Our own personal items had been removed to the British consulate for protection, but all foreign embassies and consulates were attacked and looted. The one positive piece of news was that many Arabic Bibles and Christian videos were also taken. We could only hope that God would use them to change lives.

It was a great relief to find that the Ethiopian believers we had left behind were all safe, although some had been through harrowing experiences. Our two villa security guards, Danny and Lagessa, were in particular need. They had tried to protect the house until driven off by armed men. With nowhere to go and very little money they were arrested and accused of being "spies", then thrown into jail and their remaining money stolen. When water supplies were cut off, they survived by catching water dripping from air conditioners. When power was cut off they had nothing to drink for days, in temperatures of 46°C.

I called Bishop John Brown and told him that everything was gone, and there was no money in the bank to start again.

"My dear Tom," he responded gently, "Have you lost your vision?"

"No, I haven't. But this is the reality we face."

"If you can find a place to stay…" John began, and I knew then that we were going to rebuild. Edna and I found another villa without many furnishings and used one large room as a chapel. Danny and Lagessa lived on the premises once more as guards, gardeners, and leaders of the Ethiopian church group.

The majority of foreign businesses and oil companies had pulled out of the country. Relief agencies were returning, however, and the new governor and religious court gave permission for our church project to proceed. Since we had accommodation and a place for services, we decided that finishing the clinic would have to be the next priority in spite of the fact that building material costs had increased 20 to 30 per cent. The foundations were already in place, as were 2-foot-high brick walls.

After some months Bishop John sent Revd Jim and Carol Wakerley to relieve us and take over the challenge, giving us a much needed rest back in Cyprus. Being energetic Australians they immediately got stuck in and appointed a local man as administrator to deal with all the many questions of government ministry departments, and medical supplies coming in for the clinics.

They were soon going full steam ahead, seeing miracle after miracle of God's provision. By March 1996 the clinic as well as accommodation for the medical staff had been completed. Repairs and renovation were also progressing on the church and community centre, which occupied half of the church premises. An upper floor was built with lovely bedrooms, showers, and toilet facilities. Another couple later came to relieve the Wakerleys, from the Reformed Church of America, which had a large, effective ministry in Oman. Revd Roger and Adilee Bruggink were a hard-working, happy couple who gave their all. Many continue to speak of them with gratitude and affection. Edna and I also returned at times to lend further help.

I remember that once during this time of reconstruction I was arrested and told to report to a certain colonel who was head of interior security. I protested that I was too busy with the clinics but the soldiers insisted. When I entered the colonel's office he pointed at several bags full of books.

"You are in trouble," he declared. "Look at those books. Those are from your church and you've been giving them to Muslims."

"No, Colonel. Some men have been coming into the church and taking them from the tables. I have seen six Muslim men come to the service we hold on Fridays and sit in the back. Was I supposed to tell them they couldn't come?"

"No, of course not!" shouted the colonel. "They are my men! I send them to spy on you!"

"Then those are the ones who took the books. Your men."

"Let's forget about it," he replied abruptly with a smile. "Have a coffee."

"Colonel, I never preach against Islam or against your country in the church, you ask them. I only preach from the Injil what Isa (Jesus) said and taught."

"I have a problem, Mr Thomas. I have many men and their families but no medical clinic. Could you open one for us?"

I said I could, for perhaps two or three hours per week, because we had so much else to do. He agreed. After that all went amicably. We became good friends.

Mother Teresa's sisters opened a hospice for the elderly in another part of Aden. The three of them rose at 4:30 every morning and worked until 10 p.m., caring selflessly for their scores of patients and sharing about Jesus. They were our friends and we helped whenever we could by donating surplus food or drugs.

One day a fanatic laid in wait for these women. When the three left their sleeping quarters very early in the morning to enter the hospice, they were slain. One woman's body was riddled with nineteen bullets. The Roman Catholic priest and a senior sister from India along with others, including myself, buried the women together in the only Christian cemetery in Yemen, while a strange cloud hovered over the city. The service was attended by representatives from every foreign embassy in the capital city of Sana'a, as well as Aden. It was one of the saddest days of my life. Edna and I had loved these selfless sisters of mercy.

In 2002 other Christian medical staff in the American Baptist Hospital in Jibla were also slaughtered. For over forty years the hospital had been a wonderful work of compassion and care for thousands of Yemenis. In 2009, nine foreign Christian staff and family members of a hospital in Saada,

North Yemen, were abducted. The bodies of three nurses were found shot, execution style, as was a British colleague. Two little daughters of a German couple were found alive on the border by Saudi security forces and are being brought up by their grandparents in Europe; the deaths of their parents and baby brother were only confirmed five years later. This is the high cost of commitment of service to our Lord.

Not only Westerners have paid the price. Among the labourers we hired to work on our compound was a Muslim from Guinea in West Africa. Seven years before, Vincent (as we'll call him here) had virtually walked across the continent of West Africa to the Indian Ocean in Somalia, where he found a trafficker who said he would take him by boat to Saudi Arabia. All Muslims considered this destination the land of milk and honey. He and his companions in the boat were confident they could all find good jobs there, which would allow them to send money back to their poverty-stricken families.

Like so many other trafficking victims, however, the passengers were dumped into the sea two miles off the coast of Yemen and told to swim. The majority drowned, of course. At one point the American Embassy actually called me about this tragic situation.

"You're the chaplain there in Aden, aren't you, Tom?" they asked.

"Yes," I returned, "I'm the only Protestant chaplain here."

"What are you going to do about the two hundred bodies floating in the bay?" they wanted to know.

Obviously I had no power to do anything, so the Americans sent a ship and put those men, women, and children into body bags, then buried them at sea. I take my hat off to the Americans, who are often criticized. They have compassion and take action against evil. However, the deaths continued – and still do – because of the greed of Muslim traffickers from Somalia.

Fortunately, Vincent managed to make it to land. He was put into a refugee centre and after registering he was allowed out. Spotting a building with a cross on the roof, he asked to go into our church compound. He had been told a cross meant the place was owned by Christians, and that they often helped people because they had compassion. So Vincent presented himself in rags to me, begging for food. Edna and I prayed about it and she said to me, "Take him on, there's something special about that man."

We had told Vincent that if we hired him he would be required to attend the seven o'clock prayer time every morning before starting work. He never missed one. He knew a few tribal languages of Africa, but was fluent in French and had also learned Arabic. Now he was speaking poor English. After obtaining an Injil from us he needed counsel in understanding it.

Around this time the Lord brought to Christ Church a godly couple who had been missionaries in Bhutan for many years. Drs John and Muriel Berkeley, originally from Scotland, were both trained consultants. They helped to establish the clinics with a pharmacy and proper administration. Muriel was fluent in French and had a French language Bible. She encouraged Vincent to study with her and gradually he opened his heart to Jesus. There was great joy among all the staff when he was secretly baptized in the Red Sea.

One morning Vincent came a few minutes early for devotions, and happened upon a black carryall that appeared to have been abandoned on the church grounds between the church and clinics. He looked inside the bag but did not recognize the contents for what it was: a ticking bomb, timed to go off exactly when the clinics were full of mothers and children. Vincent picked the bag up and took it over to the guard at the gate.

"Look, Ali! There's a clock in here. Must be something the pastors wanted to teach the time to children."

"It's a bomb!" screamed Ali, promptly leaping the 8-foot wall and running away as far as he could.

Vincent, only a very young, new Christian prayed, "Lord Jesus, please don't let this bomb go off." He then walked through the main gate to place the bomb in a government rubbish skip about 100 yards away where it would do no harm. The bomb disposal men were alerted and came to disarm it. Vincent had to go into hiding immediately. It turned out that extremists had planted five bombs around Aden; ours was the only one that didn't go off. Unfortunately Vincent was falsely accused of planting the bomb; he was tortured and imprisoned for four months.

I should add here this was not to be the only bomb attack on our church property. Another attempt was made in November 1998 by eight British Muslims who travelled to Yemen with specific instructions to bomb the church and clinics, as well as the British Consulate. Fortunately this bomb too was discovered just in time. The eight men, trained in terrorist camps which were sponsored by al-Qaeda, were arrested and found guilty.

Ironically, our clinic staff did prison medical work and

actually treated some of the attackers. When one asked a nurse where she was from and why she was working in Aden, she replied, "I work at the church and clinic you came to bomb!"

Stunned, the man had to admit, "I need a brain scan."

A few years later on 1 January 2001 a bomb did explode beside the staff accommodation building, leaving three flats unliveable and removing about 6 metres of the 8-foot-high boundary wall. The church windows were also damaged, but by the grace of God no one was killed or injured.

One day after our friend Vincent's release from prison, officials broke into his room and found his Bible. He admitted freely that he had been a Muslim but had become a Christian.

"No! You were born a Muslim, so you are still a Muslim," they insisted.

They flogged Vincent but he refused to deny his faith, so they arrested him again. I was quite frantic, trying to trace which prison they had put him into. No one would tell me and every door seemed firmly closed. Through a sympathetic Muslim man, however, I finally learned where he was and drove six and a half hours into the mountains to visit this brother, taking along some basic provisions. I was shocked to find him living in appalling conditions, packed into a small cell that held about forty others. A hole in the floor served as the toilet and there was a tap for water, but the cell had absolutely no light except for the little that came through the bars of the iron door. Some men had been incarcerated for two or three years in that place, without a trial. Almost all were covered with skin diseases because of the filth they were forced to live in. The stench was overpowering.

When I saw Vincent through the bars I called out to him, and a smile instantly lit his face.

"Oh, Daddy Tom!" he came eagerly over to talk to me. "This place is the will of God for me."

I was deeply affected, wondering if I were in his situation, I could declare so cheerfully that this hole in the ground was God's will.

The second thing he said to me was, "Did you bring my Bible?"

The police had left his Bible in the room and only taken his passport. When I squeezed the book through the bars and he held it in his hands once again he was overjoyed. "They all know here that I'm a Christian. Now I can show them the true way to God."

Later it struck me that the Muslim prisoners in that cell could easily kill Vincent, but this brother was fearless for Jesus Christ.

Edna insisted on going with me for the second visit. I tried to dissuade her but she would not be moved. We loaded up with medical supplies this time. About fifteen minutes away from the prison Edna remarked that she could smell chicken being roasted on a spit. True enough, there on the roadside was a little man roasting chickens and baking flat bread to sell. We purchased twenty chickens, split them into halves and wrapped them in the bread. The authorities were amazed that two Europeans, one of them a woman at that, would not only care enough about a prisoner to visit him, but bring hot meals for all the rest. When Vincent saw Edna, the tears flowed. He has always loved her as a son would his mother.

But the hand of God was truly on that young man.

Although he was considered an infidel and only worthy of death in that culture, he not only survived, but brought many others to faith in Jesus Christ.

I went to the UN's refugee agency (UNHCR) to tell them that Vincent was being persecuted because he was a Christian, and he shouldn't be in prison. The staff person I talked to noted that his superiors were all Muslims, so it wouldn't be easy. According to the tenets of Islam, Vincent was an infidel and deserved to die. I argued that the staff of the UNHCR were supposed to be impartial. If Vincent wasn't released I would fly to Geneva in seven days' time and personally present his case at the UNHCR headquarters. I knew all of the Aden staff members' names and would report a miscarriage of justice. I would also report it to the British press.

Within twenty-four hours the agency was on the phone to me. They would release Vincent from prison if I could find a country that would take him. I would also have to give them $2,000 for a plane ticket. Of course, it was the UNHCR that should pay and make such arrangements, but it was a bit of a hot potato to find a country in the West willing to take a Muslim-background Christian. Eventually, however, our organization found a Bible school in South Africa that agreed to enrol Vincent. I raised the necessary money but refused to pay the UNHCR, buying the plane ticket myself. On the way south his plane stopped in Nairobi and he was arrested again – so again we had to pay a ransom to speed him on his way.

Vincent had given us a moving letter to read to the church in Yemen, knowing it was unlikely he would ever see them again. He thanked his brothers and sisters warmly for their kindness and their prayers during his ordeal, through which God had given him the strength to share about Christ. He also pleaded with them to keep on loving one other.

Letters continued to come to Edna and me from South Africa, thanking his "Mom and Dad" as he always called us, for investing in him. During his studies he took every opportunity to take the gospel door-to-door and to the open markets, visiting Hindus and Muslims in Durban and elsewhere. He also urged churches to get involved with Muslim evangelism.

Vincent had the option of going to live in one of five European countries after he finished his time at the Bible school, but he refused, saying he needed to go to "his own Jerusalem". He went back to Guinea to share the good news of Christ among the unreached Muslims of his own country.

In 2007 I spent eight days in that part of Africa to see his work. "When this Muslim convert came to our church, the Holy Spirit came with him," Vincent's pastor told me. "We were slumbering until he joined us. He couldn't understand why so few of our members attended prayer meetings. Now we have all-night prayer meetings, and many go."

Vincent also served as a translator for services in his evangelical church. He and his team routinely fasted each Friday before attending prayer meetings, which lasted from 10 p.m. to 6 a.m. Then they washed, ate a very small breakfast, and went out again all day Saturday to evangelize Muslims.

Edna and I felt privileged over the next years to help raise funds for a mission house in Guinea, a place that could also serve as a refuge for new, Muslim-background believers. Altogether Vincent and his wife Suzanne started four churches while evangelizing scores of villages in the interior, leading many Muslims to faith in Christ. At the time of this writing even more have responded.

I had the great joy of baptizing other Muslim-background believers who worked for us in Yemen. Following this biblical precept was a critical step in their new faith, although they knew it might well lead to martyrdom.

We did medical and practical work among the thousands who lived in Yemen's largest Somali refugee camp, near Aden. One dear little child died in my arms, she was so emaciated. When we took her to the *imam* to be buried he refused to take her, unless he was paid £16. Muslims wouldn't bury people who died of AIDS, either, so we took care of them. The bodies were dumped outside our church and clinics.

I was shaken when another child in the camp, only seven, cried out in fear as I approached him to dress his wounds and wash his hair.

"Are you going to kill me? Please don't kill me!"

This boy was still traumatized from seeing his parents and many others killed back in Somalia. Love and gentleness finally won him over, and he sat contentedly on my lap. As we cuddled each other I had a lump in my throat. I wished we could adopt him.

A few of the young Somali refugees who put their trust in Jesus when they worked with us were imprisoned and tortured. George (not his birth name) was offered many bribes to return to Islam, but when he refused to renounce his faith he was sentenced to death. His wife Sara was also beaten, but not imprisoned because of their eleven-month-old son. At that time Pastor Roger and his wife were serving for a year in Aden. They applied to the UNHCR to get this brother's release and when he went on leave I attended court and continued to appeal for access to George, to no avail. After that we were targeted for malicious lies in the national press and from preachers in the mosques. Then, without warning, the local chief of police and a colonel in immigration walked into the church compound and ordered me to dismiss four members of our staff within the hour. These were our Christian Ethiopian staff members, and to lose them so quickly would have crippled us all since they did essential cleaning and maintenance work.

I engaged in some strong conversation with these gentlemen and obtained three days' grace. We used the time to appeal to the governor of Aden, an old friend, as well as the director general of immigration and British consul. We were prepared to go higher, but thankfully the order was rescinded.

Baroness Cox of Christian Solidarity Worldwide in the UK also worked on George's behalf, and praise God he was freed three days before his execution was due to be carried out. He and Sara are now living in New Zealand, attending a good fellowship and still witnessing boldly for God.

Another Somali man who wanted to be called David after his conversion went on to establish evangelistic ministries in both Yemen and Ethiopia, among the Somalis there. I clearly recall one occasion the day after a particular worship meeting that David gently rebuked me. "Why did you close the service last night when the Holy Spirit was so evidently with us?"

"Our nurses have to get up so early. They were tired. I was tired too," I explained.

He went on, "When we went back to our room we fell

on our knees. The Spirit was so strong as we continued to worship! First one man, and then another, began to speak in lovely unknown languages. We never heard of this before. Why did you never tell us that those who worship can receive new languages?" he asked in wonder.

I felt humbled, and apologized for the lack of teaching on this subject. I said that we would definitely begin to study the gifts of the Spirit.

David left his mark for the Lord whom he loved and served so fearlessly. After over nine years in Yemen things became too hot for him. We hid him for three months and then managed to get him to Ethiopia, via Djibouti. There he began to share Jesus with the 600,000 or more Somalis that had come over the border. He found a small room to rent in a densely populated area with many living in deep poverty. Soon it had to be two rooms and they were like a spiritual GP's practice, full of people every day of the week. David also had a big heart for the widows and children of Christian martyrs, caring for them and sometimes going without food himself to feed them. David's enemies once stabbed him seven times in the head, hands, and chest, and while he was in hospital his landlord re-let his rooms. Half his possessions were stolen.

When I went to see Vincent (mentioned above) in Guinea in 2007, I also visited David in Ethiopia. He needed Somali Bibles, so we had managed to get three hundred sent from Denmark, at a much lower cost than they were in the UK. Some of these Bibles were smuggled by hand into Somalia itself, at great risk.

Many Somalis had turned from Islam to Christ. David introduced me to some of those who were now leading

Bible cell groups themselves. I asked one man, named Ali, how long he had been a Christian and he said eight months.

"I was approached by David. He has a very confrontational approach, you know!" He grinned. "'I understand that you are well known in various mosques,' David said to me. 'You sing the Quran. You are singing deceit, do you know that? I was a Muslim myself, but I found the truth. Here. Read this Injil.' I was disturbed as I read the Injil. One night after going to sleep, Jesus appeared to me in a dream. I went to ask David if he knew of anyone else who had seen Jesus in a dream, and he said yes, many others. Jesus sometimes reveals Himself to people in dreams."

Ali put his faith in Jesus and began fearlessly telling other Muslims about Him. He sat down with his two wives and seven children and read the gospel to them. They too received Jesus Christ into their lives. Now Ali sings a new song – the songs of Zion.

Edna and I loved David like a son, but he is now with the many souls in heaven who are clothed in white robes, worshipping before their Lord.[6] David was brutally martyred in April 2008, at the age of thirty-two, when he went to visit his aging mother who was ill and who he hadn't seen in ten years. In our last conversation he told me the Holy Spirit had confirmed to him that he should get all his family together in Somalia, and he should lovingly share the gospel of Jesus Christ. This he did, and every day for two weeks his relatives sat and listened as he opened the Bible to them.

Sadly, his own sister betrayed him. David's killers came with automatic weapons and dragged his bullet-riddled body

6 Revelation 6:6–11

through the streets, shouting that an infidel was dead. They even put his body on display outside a mosque so that more people could view it and rejoice. Finally, they abandoned David's remains on a rubbish heap.

Besides the refugees in Yemen who were attracted to Christ, we constantly met Yemenis with a deep hunger to know more about Isa (Jesus). Several men approached me in various places to share that they needed the Injil or complete Bible, adding that they truly believed in Isa. In a market area men often sidled up to me while Edna was busy, to confide that they wished the British were back in control of Aden, for then they went to church with no fear at all, and believed in Jesus. One man unashamedly repeated the Lord's Prayer to me, pronouncing every word perfectly and meaningfully. He told me he prayed it every day.

Another typical experience was the conversation Edna and I had with a young man we met one day while walking along the Steamer Point pier in Aden. He asked if we were tourists.

"No, we work here," we told him.

"Where?"

"The *kanisa* (church)."

"Oh, really?" His face brightened with excitement. "Would you be able to give me the Injil, please? The one copy I had I gave to my Syrian friend, who pleaded for it."

From the bag we always carried we gave him a dual translation of the New Testament, and enjoyed a lengthy conversation.

On another Sunday morning when we went to the telecommunications centre in the city, to make our usual weekly five-minute call to our daughter, Sharon, in the UK, the employee behind the counter pointed to the Quran he had with him.

"I don't imagine you know what this is," he stated confidently.

"Oh yes I do; it is the Quran," I replied.

"You have not read it?"

I quoted two verses from the book, and his eyebrows shot up in surprise.

Then I reached into my bag and pulled out a New Testament. "But have you read this Book, the holy Injil?"

Before he could reply another man behind the counter shouted, "The holy Injil! Is it really the Injil in Arabic? You must give it to me, please. I have wanted to read it for a long time."

A crowd gathered, questions were asked about several issues, and more New Testaments were given out. After that encounter we had opportunities to distribute even more copies, and the man who waited so long for one received extra copies for friends who began reading it together.

In an office that belonged to a member of our Christian fellowship, I met a Muslim employee sitting behind a typewriter.

"I have a question that I've always wanted answered," this lady confided. "You, being a priest, will tell me the truth. Is it true that our Prophet is mentioned in the Gospels?"

"No, madam, it is not true," I replied.

"But we are told by our *mullahs* that it is true."

"Then your *mullahs* don't tell the truth, or they speak out of ignorance."

"Is your Gospel the true Gospel, and not changed?" she then asked. Most Muslims believe that the Christian Bible has been changed by its many versions and is no longer faithful to the original text.

"Yes, it is, and it is over five hundred years older than the Quran; it is a true translation."

The lady looked me squarely in the eyes. "I believe you. We must talk about this again."

I could relate dozens of similar conversations that betray a great hunger and thirst for spiritual truth in this part of the world.

A sheikh once told me privately, "Thomas, my friend, I am praying that Christianity will become more and more powerful in this region and all of the Middle East. We need more people like you and your wife to live among us. Our people need to know who Jesus is and what is true Christianity. Thomas, a time is coming – it will be with great power. Pray and wait for it. Be patient for it will surely come, my friend."

That sounded like a prophecy to me. We had held several long discussions with this man and he had accepted the Arabic Bible and *Jesus* film. Afterwards he telephoned to say he was blessed by the film and was gathering some of his friends to see it, as well as share the reading of his Bible. We are convinced that he was a secret believer.

All who visit the Arab world can find evidence of the marvellous impact of God's Word. Often Muslims are first exposed to it through Christian radio or TV broadcasts or the Internet.

On one occasion I went into a city bank that I had frequented several times before in Yemen, and waited with a number of other customers to transact my business. Arab banks are not like English banks; nobody stands in orderly queues. It's chaos, at least in most I have entered. Everyone tries to push and shove their way to the counter at the same time.

While I was standing there, carrying, as usual, my two bags of Bibles, the assistant manager spotted me and cried, "Ha! Mr Thomas!"

"Hello," I acknowledged the man, smiling.

"Mr Thomas, you are a priest. Yes?"

"Yes," I agreed, since Revelation 5:10 clearly implies that God commissions His children to act as priests in His kingdom.

The man immediately proclaimed to everyone within earshot who I was. Then he announced, "Mr Thomas, I am an empty, empty Muslim. How can I become a Christian?"

I was nonplussed that he would make such a statement and ask such a question in the middle of a busy bank, surrounded by a sea of interested listeners. But I told this manager, "My friend, you really need to read the holy Injil, the gospel of Jesus, for yourself."

"Ha!" He exclaimed in despair. "How can I get a copy of this Injil? You cannot get it in this country!"

"Well, it so happens," I reached into one of my bags, "I have a copy for you here."

The bank manager reached over the heads of the people in front of me and took it.

"This is truly the Injil?"

"Yes. It is."

"Look!" he shouted gleefully, displaying the Book to his assistants and tellers. "This is the true Injil! It's in Arabic!" (Most Arabs seem to think that if something is printed in Arabic it has to be true.) He was so excited that everyone else in the bank began immediately to clamour for a copy. Within minutes all 20 kilos that I had in my bags vanished. Some of the customers offered to buy the Books, though I kept telling them they were free. Several told me that they listened to a Christian radio programme.

Every time I went to the bank after this experience, I was besieged with requests for more Injils. All because Christian broadcasts had sowed the seeds of curiosity and paved the way.

Sadly, I have also met up with foreigners in Yemen who come from Christian backgrounds but are now lost in "enemy" territory. The wife of the British Ambassador, during one period that we lived there, voluntarily became a Muslim. Others are not such willing recruits.

Once I was requested to substitute for the consul for a couple of days at the British Consulate in Aden, when he had to be away. I was sitting in his office when the Muslim assistant came in to say there was a lady outside the gate. Apparently she had a problem he couldn't handle.

"Can she speak English?" I asked. He said yes, so I directed him to let her through security to see me.

A female veiled in black from head to foot came into the office with a little boy. I asked her to sit down and spoke gently, trying to put her at ease.

"I hear you have a problem. Can I help?"

I could see that she was shaking and sobbing behind her veil.

"Take your time. I'll get you a glass of water."

She tore off the veil then, and I saw an American girl sitting in front of me. The girl told me that she had been born and brought up in the United States, but when she was sixteen or seventeen her Yemeni parents had told her they were all going to Yemen to visit relatives. What she wasn't told was that only two of their three tickets were return. Her own flight was one-way. She was forced into marriage and raped within twenty-four hours of landing in Yemen.

"Please," she wept, "can you help me? I don't have much time. I'm only allowed one hour a week out of the house. *Please!*"

"Have you got your American passport?" I asked the girl. She nodded and fumbled in her clothing before passing it over to me.

I took down the details and returned the passport. There was no American Embassy in Aden but I told her I would see that her case reached the embassy.

"But let me warn you," I added. "You won't be able to take your little boy with you if you leave."

Her sobbing became uncontrollable. "He was born of rape. But I love him!"

I was gripped with compassion as the girl hurried away with her little son, the white trainers on her feet just visible under her black *abaya*.

A friend came into the office shortly afterwards and remarked on my sad expression.

"You'd be unhappy too if you just heard the story I heard," I said, and gave him a summary of what had transpired.

The man jumped to his feet. "I've got two or three thousand dollars in my pocket!" he cried. "I must find her! I could help her, and get her across the Red Sea to freedom. I have contacts."

"Look for a woman with white running shoes!" I shouted after him as he dashed away. Sadly, my friend returned defeated and dripping with perspiration after about forty minutes. The girl had been lost in the crowd of faceless, black-covered women on the streets. Although I was able to pass her details to some concerned Americans, I heard no more.

Another case very like this was brought to my attention. A nurse attached to our soon-to-open medical clinic found a young English Muslim teenager sitting on the steps outside the British Consulate, crying his heart out. It was on a Friday, the Muslim holy day, so all offices, embassies, and other public places were closed. She came to see me afterwards.

"Tom, you need to go around to the British Consulate. There's a British teenager on the steps there saying something about his sister being held against her will."

I did not delay but went to find the boy. He was still sitting there dejectedly, holding his head in his hands.

"Hello, young man," I said. "I'm afraid no embassy or businesses are open today, but they will be tomorrow."

"I need help now! My parents tricked my sister. She is being kept in a mountain village against her will and is to be forced into a marriage!"

As I sat with him the boy revealed how his mother and father, back in the UK, had told his younger sister that they were going to visit her grandparents and other family members in Yemen, where they originated. After a few weeks' holiday they would return to Cardiff. His sister was excited to go, never dreaming that her father had arranged for her to be married to a man almost twice her age. Her parents had now returned home without her. The boy, who had not been invited on the trip, was horrified. He loved his sister deeply. He made up his mind to travel to Yemen and find her and bring her back to Cardiff.

I felt righteous anger stir within me as he recounted the story, and my heart went out to him. I suggested that he should return to the UK as soon as possible and contact one or two national newspapers. He did just that. The *Daily Express* not only published the deceitful action of the parents but flew out a reporter and photographers to Yemen. They found where the girl was held captive, and made the story into a double spread in the paper. They were able to take her home and she was reunited with her brother − but not her father. When he was interviewed by the press he asked for £10,000 before telling his side of the story. They politely (I think!) told him where to go.

Edna and I say well done to The *Daily Express* for going to those lengths and rescuing this young girl. For her, at least, the story ended happily, though it does not for many others.

I remember the time I was walking along the street in a nearby country, en route to the airport, when a woman veiled in black came up beside me and whispered urgently, "Are you English? Help me! Oh, please! I come from Sheffield."

"Can't the British Embassy help you?"

"No. They don't or won't help me and my husband has my passport. Please. I must get away! I met a handsome Arab student at university in Sheffield. He loved partying and we fell in love and he persuaded me to come here and marry, which I did, and oh how I regret it. He is unfaithful and I am just a slave in effect." She was crying by this time.

"The British Embassy *must* help you; you must make a nuisance of yourself to them," I urged. I was catching a flight so could not delay, but sought to encourage the woman not to give up.

Many young ladies in England seem mesmerized by the Muslim foreign students they meet, and visualize happy-ever-after marriages with their prince charmings. These girls grew up without much interest in Christianity or the church; some have never even entered one. Yet thousands are willing to embrace Islam, which they know little or nothing about because a handsome, high flying, party-going Arab comes on to them and says all they have to do is say a few words (which the *imam* will help them with), and they'll be okay. The reality is tragically different.

Although non-Muslim girls may marry Muslim men, the reverse is never allowed. The reason is that marrying non-Muslim girls is seen as a way to proselytize them and bring them under the rule of Islam. Brides soon learn that they have surrendered their freedom and bought into a rigidly controlled system that is hard for them – or their children – to escape. In fact, it is not unheard of for Muslim husbands to suddenly remove the children and whisk them back to their home countries to live. The mothers may never see them again. Several gripping, true stories about such marriages are listed in the appendix at the end of this book.

9
YEMEN: DIVINE APPOINTMENTS

During the years that we were based in Yemen, Edna and I travelled to Singapore to challenge Christians on that island nation to consider working in the Middle East. We spoke one evening in a very large Anglican church which had a congregation of about a thousand. Among those present was a young Chinese nurse named Patricia who had already worked in Saudi Arabia. Just before the service began this young woman prayed, "Lord, if this man speaks about Yemen I will know you want me to return to the Middle East."

Of course, when I got up I began at once to talk about the needs of Yemen. Afterwards Patricia came to share her heart with Edna and me, and we counselled her. She kept her promise to the Lord and with her church's support went out to join the clinic staff on our church compound. The Yemeni women and children loved her. I think she was the first Chinese that many had ever met! But she spoke Arabic and everyone naturally gravitated towards her.

After four years of serving in the clinic Patricia decided to go up to the mountains to do medical work in villages where they'd never seen a doctor or nurse. She had the same impact there, and was greatly loved by the people. She was also able to distribute Gospels in Arabic to those she met.

One early morning in 2005 we received the news that Patricia had been killed in a road accident in the mountains. Edna and I wept, for this girl was like another daughter to us and she had called us her English mother and father. She had written earlier that she had received threats to her life, so we do not know the whole story. Some things remain a mystery. But so often it is single ladies who obey God's call and follow Him to hard places. We need to pray more for them, and for all who go in obedience to serve in the Muslim world.

I have mentioned some of the others who have been brutally martyred in Yemen, in both North and South. Some individuals we knew personally, others by name, faithfully working among the Yemeni people because they loved them. We honour their memory and pray for the friends and family who will always miss them.

In the previous chapter I recounted how a wonderful couple from New Zealand, Jim and Carol Wakerley, took over the Aden project from Edna and me early in 1995. I was delighted to be able to return and participate in the dedication of the restored church in 1997. On that occasion Bishop Clive Handford asked if Edna and I could return to Aden in February the next year for perhaps six months, when the Wakerleys were due to leave.

We agreed. In addition to serving as pastor and project director of the clinic, I also acted as honorary chaplain to the hundreds of seamen who visited the busy port of Aden. The problems of these seafarers from Sudan, Somalia, Ethiopia, Cameroon, Romania, and other countries often seemed overwhelming. Some went unpaid for months or even years and were abandoned in Yemen, unable to return to their homes. Most had families they had not seen in years.

It took careful diplomacy with various authorities to obtain renewal of passports and other travel documents. Meanwhile, the Mission to Seafarers in London kindly advanced money so that we could feed and water the distressed men. When we learned of a group of Muslim sailors stranded in another port, we provided their daily food for three and a half months and visited them every week, although it meant a return trip of 60 miles. The men called us their father and mother and said they knew we loved them, adding, "Nobody has cared for us except you."

Soon they all had copies of the precious Book of books and were reading about the One who loved them more than anyone else. Eventually they were allowed to go home.

I enjoyed driving into the port area and parking my car near the gangways of ships, meeting people from many nations and often having the chance to share my faith. One time after spending two hours visiting various ships, the security guard forbade me to go on the Saudi ship because they were "not good people". I argued that I went on every ship but he insisted that I must not go on that one.

Another time my car was stopped by an aggressive soldier at the seaport main gate who refused to recognize my official pass. He pointed his gun in my direction and escorted me to an office where two officers examined the pass and questioned what I did on the ships. I told them that I was a "Christian *imam* (priest)", because I knew they would understand that term. One of the men insisted that he would stay with me to listen to what I said to the passengers.

After two hours of visiting ships I returned to my car to drive it off. However, the same soldier who had been with me all the time directed me to pull over to a quiet spot.

"What present are you going to give me?" he asked, looking me right in the eye.

I was sure the man expected a bribe. "What kind of gift do you want?" I enquired.

He smiled. "The holy Injil and Torah." Pointing to his heart, he then revealed, "Jesus is in here."

This man had been a secret believer for years; only now, when we were alone, did he dare to confide the truth to me. I gladly gave the officer the six copies of the Bible that he said he could use, plus other books and the *Jesus* film in Arabic. Then he asked when I would be coming through again. I was to bring six more copies each time.

When I asked why, he simply said, "There are many of us."

I was only able to scratch the surface of what could be done in Yemen's busy ports, of course. Often I pleaded with others to pray with me for a full-time worker. In fact, the international Mission to Seafarers moved to establish a ministry off the coast of the United Arab Emirates, in 2006. The city of Fujairah on the Gulf of Oman hosts the second largest bunker (refuelling) anchorage in the world. Between a hundred to a hundred and fifty ships are anchored there at any given time and over 10,500 ships are refuelled annually. Many seamen do not get ashore. The Mission launched an "Angel Appeal" to build and equip the first seafarer support boat of its kind in the world. Today the MV *Flying Angel* operates seven days a week, providing email and telephone facilities as well as a book and DVD library, shop, and chaplain.

Living in Yemen often provided surprising contacts with other expatriates. One time I was the only Westerner in the check-in lounge at Aden Airport, waiting for a flight to the capital city, when a fine-looking Chinese lady appeared with two Chinese men. The latter accompanied the lady to the first class check-in desk, and after putting her cases on the weighing machine, bowed their heads slightly and left. As the lady was dealing with her ticket I clearly heard the gentle voice of God's Spirit within me say, *Speak to her about Me.*

Immediately my inborn nature responded, *You can't! She is in first class and you will be sitting in economy.* However, I did tell myself that if the Lord wanted me to speak to the woman about Him, He would get me upgraded to first class.

After boarding the plane I found my window seat and settled down with two empty seats beside me. Suddenly I saw the Chinese lady being escorted from first class by a male steward. He placed her in the aisle seat of my row. She seemed very angry. Inwardly I told the Lord that I would certainly speak to this passenger about Him, once we were in the air.

Then the same steward came down the aisle again, pushing forward a male passenger. He indicated that the Chinese lady should move into the middle seat, next to me. This upset her even more.

"These people, they have no manners!" she exclaimed, venting her disgust. "Look. I have a first class seat and I am a Chinese diplomat. I should be in first class but they put me out because I was the only female there, and made me sit here."

"Yes, they can seem difficult at times," I responded soothingly, "but they have cultural restrictions. Men and women eat and socialize in separate rooms."

"Then you should be in the first class with the men, and

so should all the other men! It's nonsense, that's what it is."

She was obviously still heated about the arrangement so I could only smile as we took to the air. After a while she asked me if I was American or British, and what I was doing in Aden. That opened the door. I told her why Edna and I were working in the city. Then I explained how we had come to know Jesus Christ as a personal Saviour and how we had become new people, with transformed delights and desires. I shared about our ministry in Singapore and Hong Kong among members of the British military, and our centre on an island off Hong Kong called Hey Ling Chau. She listened, fascinated, as I described the island as a former home for lepers from the mainland of China, and where a Scottish surgeon and his staff had gone to serve after being put out of China.

The lady looked at me thoughtfully for a moment and then hung her head. I knew that she too had a story to tell.

"When I was eight years old, living with my parents and grandparents, the government said that I had to be removed from my home to Peking (now Beijing). I was to be educated in the new philosophy and political thinking. My family were good Christian Presbyterians and we wept when we were parted. I never saw them again."

I felt a lump in my throat, deeply moved. It was obvious to me that the little girl had been taken away to be brainwashed by the Communist regime.

She wiped tears from her eyes as I said, "I am sure that your parents and grandparents never forgot you, and a day never passed that they didn't pray for you."

"They are now dead, except for my grandmother who is very old and waiting for death herself. I was taught that the British were arrogant, ignorant people who lost their empire because of their moral weaknesses and wickedness. But I can tell that you are the opposite of that, and a true Christian."

The plane landed in Sana'a and we all stood up to collect our luggage. It was raining heavily. Once we were inside the terminal building the lady asked, "Have you a car?"

I told her that I would be catching a taxi into the city.

"You need not. My husband has the embassy car and he will take you wherever you wish to go. I will introduce you."

This she did. Once I had the rest of my luggage we got into an impressive black car with the flag of China flapping in the breeze. I sat in back and they sat together in front. The rain and wind increased as we proceeded along the highway, and suddenly a car shot out of a side road. The two Yemeni men inside were chewing qat,[7] not paying attention, and we crashed although our driver tried to avoid it.

The husband jumped out of the car and let off steam, shouting at the Yemeni men. A crowd soon gathered, over twenty or more Yemeni men in the pouring rain. I tried to calm the gentleman and his wife, and as I did so an old Yemeni man said to me in English, "Get your friend away quickly."

---

7 Qat is a green plant widely grown in Yemen, a narcotic with many of the effects of amphetamine. Because it suppresses hunger, addicts often become anorexic and malnourished and vulnerable to diseases like high blood pressure, hypertension, gastrointestinal problems, periodontal disease, and even cancer of the oesophagus. Each day from about noon to 4 p.m., Yemeni shops close and life grinds to a halt as 85 per cent of men and 35 per cent of women join the communal ritual of qat-chewing. It is so much a part of the culture that few Yemenis could contemplate life without it. It is not uncommon for pregnant women to pass along their addiction to their newborn babies. Qat is quite legal in Yemen and one of its major unofficial exports.

There was no car insurance in Yemen, so I put a restraining arm on the driver. "It is best we go quickly. I will write a testimonial for your ambassador, explaining the accident and saying you were not to blame."

The man's wife was also seeking to quiet him. We got back into the car and I sent a quick prayer to the Lord to make it move and get us away from this unfriendly mob. Yemeni men traditionally wear a large, curved dagger tucked into an ornate belt, which adds to their fierce appearance. I wouldn't have given much for our chances if they had closed ranks against the foreigners.

The car began to move but the gentleman was still raging, so I put a hand on each shoulder from behind and said, "My friend, we are alive, not dead. God has delivered us."

His wife interpreted the words I spoke and she smiled at me. He eventually calmed down and took me to the home of a Dutch family where I was staying. As we shook hands, the lady thanked me and gave me their names and a personal card with their embassy address and address in China.

"Have you a Chinese Bible?" she asked.

"No, not here, but I can send one to your embassy here in Sana'a."

With that we parted.

Wout and Marina Van Dijk from the Netherlands were very special friends who served in the international school for many years. Their home was an oasis for hundreds, including Edna and myself, both physically and spiritually. Tired travellers were refreshed and those who went forth bearing precious seed received prayer, encouragement, and hospitality. They always offered me accommodation and meals whenever I was in the capital; I had stayed with them and their delightful daughters many times.

"How was the trip, Tom?" Wout enquired after we exchanged warm greetings.

"Do you really want to know?" I laughed. We sat down and while we ate dinner I told them the story, finishing up by saying that I wished I had a Chinese Bible with me. I would have to send one from Cyprus.

"But Tom," said Wout, "don't you recall that when all the hundreds of Chinese workers were here building new roads, you got in a large consignment of Chinese Bibles for us to distribute?"

I did remember. Wout and others had done a good job of sowing those Mandarin Scriptures.

"Well, we have one or two copies left, and they are on the shelf."

I had an early flight to Cyprus, so it was arranged between us that Marina would take the Bibles to the Chinese Embassy the next day. This she did, personally handing them to the diplomat, who received them graciously.

What happened after that is written in heaven. One thing we can be certain of, however, is that our meeting was no coincidence. The One who arranged it would continue to work out His purposes in that lady's life. That's the kind of caring, persevering God He is.

I had another encounter with a diplomat when I travelled in a car to the airport with John Brown, then Bishop of Cyprus and the Gulf, and the British vice-consul. The latter gentleman was a Muslim, having converted from Hinduism some thirty years previously in Yemen. As we drove along he happened to comment, "We have a book in the Quran that is my favourite, the story of Job. It has eight chapters about his life."

"In our holy Bible, sir, we have forty-two chapters about Job. Yours must be a condensed version," I responded. The bishop caught my eye and smiled.

"Really? Forty-two chapters in the Bible? I would love to read them all."

"It so happens that I have a new copy of the Arabic Bible in my briefcase. Would you like it, sir?"

"Yes, please. Indeed I would."

The man was truly delighted to accept a copy. Nearly eighteen months later when I returned to Yemen I went to the consulate to see him. This time I did not have Arabic Bibles in my briefcase but a recently produced video by MECO & Associates. This was the story of the Prodigal Son in Arabic, very well acted and an excellent tool. I had only six copies since videos were not really part of my ministry, but I had been asked on this occasion to take some with me.

As I entered the vice-consul's office he rose and kissed me on both cheeks, saying warmly, "Tom, it's good to see you. Sit down and have coffee with me."

We caught up on various news and then he suddenly said, "You remember the lovely Bible you gave me when we were travelling with Bishop John Brown?"

"Yes," I smiled. "And did you read the forty-two chapters of Job?"

He gave me a broad grin in return and laughed. "Indeed I did. They are much more informative and challenging than the eight chapters in our Quran. But I want to tell you that I think one of the most amazing stories that Jesus spoke about was the Prodigal Son. It is a lovely account of restoration. It ought to be made into a film."

Now it was my turn to be astonished. I opened my large briefcase and said, "My dear friend, here is the very film, just produced in Arabic. It is the story of the Prodigal Son."

The man was speechless for a moment. Then he cried, "Tom, this is God's goodness."

Jumping out of his seat he took me into his huge arms, hugging me and kissing my cheeks so hard I thought my cheekbone would crack. It didn't.

Later the vice-consul communicated to me through a safe channel to ask if he could have six more copies, if he covered all costs. I was able to do this and he generously reimbursed me. What thrilled me most was that this man was obviously not just reading about Job, he was also delving into the Gospels… and possibly further.

* * *

I have said little about the medical work on our church grounds in Aden, which often made the difference between life and death for local people. On most days the single doctor and nurse in charge of the clinic were overwhelmed by almost a hundred patients – 2,500 a month – yet they made time to treat others in villages and prisons and held extra clinics in Aden's Somali Refugee Camp. The United Nations' refugee agency, UNHCR, thought very highly of the work of these two women. Senior Staff Nurse Thea Groenveld, who previously worked for fourteen years at a hospital near the Saudi border before her last four years with us in Aden, was honoured by the Queen of Holland for her selfless service. The Italian government also took note of our work. The embassy gave the clinic a vehicle and came to the rescue with three months' supply of drugs when we were low in stock.

That last, seven-month stint in Yemen was something like riding a rollercoaster, with unexpected ups and downs at every turn. Easter services at Christ Church – the only Protestant church in the country – had record attendance with perhaps twenty different nationalities; something not seen since the colonial era of the 1960s. We also celebrated the baptism of three men who had come out of great darkness.

One of the British families who were with us over the Easter break was kidnapped on their way back to the airport in Sana'a. Thankfully the Mitchells were released after two weeks in the hands of rebel tribesmen. Abductions of foreigners were common, an attempt to extract money or concessions from the Yemeni government. Over a hundred people had been kidnapped within a five-year period. Yemeni believers have also disappeared.

But God arranged encouragements along our way as well and even moments of light relief. When I was invited to speak for an hour in a local school I wondered if I could hold the children's attention that long. The day after my visit I received a bundle of letters expressing their appreciation. Wrote one child, "You have been through many good and hard times, Mr Tom, and I think it's not too late for you to go into acting, you would be a wonderful actor."

Can it be that I missed my calling?

Edna and I handed over our responsibilities to replacements at the end of the summer of 1998. To this day, Christ Church and Ras Morbat Clinic in Aden continue to provide invaluable spiritual and physical aid to thousands of men, women, and children. But Yemen remains a strife-torn nation. Tribal feuds abound and in recent years al-Qaeda has made the country a training ground for rebellious Muslims. Could we be living in the period that Scriptures have foretold as the time of sorrows, with men's hearts failing them for fear?[8] I advise readers to study God's Word and decide for themselves!

8 See Matthew 24:8; Luke 21:26

10
SAUDI ARABIA: ISLAM'S GROUND ZERO

As I'd been advised when I first signed up for God's "Mission Impossible", Saudi Arabia was and still is the toughest place on the planet to courier copies of the Word of God. While some of the expatriate workers in this Islamic stronghold are Christians, there are pitifully few followers of Jesus among the Saudi population. No surprise when one considers that a Saudi Arab who converts to Christianity has a fair chance of being beheaded.

By 1987 I had made contact with some fine American believers who worked in Saudi Arabia, holding responsible positions in their respective companies. They invited me to visit the large complex of houses in which they lived. This exclusive area boasted a gated entrance and lovely, manicured grounds with a swimming pool. Their fifteen or so homes were surrounded by a 10- or 12-foot-high wall.

When I arrived, an American brother met me at the gate and escorted me to his home where over thirty people had gathered. During the refreshment time preceding our meeting he introduced me to everyone as "a man who believed God was cutting through gates of brass, to bring His Word in Arabic into the land". I shared some of my testimony before preaching about the person of Christ as Son of God and Saviour of the world, who died for all people, including Jews and Muslims.

As I drew to a close one of the group shouted out, "Now I know Jesus is my Messiah!" The man was an American Jew who had been shown the love of God by his fellow workers. These same friends had also shared insights into the Bible. But on the night of our meeting he made up his mind to let everyone know that he was putting his trust in the Son as his Saviour.

He then expressed the desire to make a further public commitment. "I must be baptized tonight!" he declared.

I looked questioningly at my host, wondering if it would be possible to use a bathroom for the purpose, and he gave me a lovely smile.

"We have a swimming pool in the complex, so why not have a baptism there? No one else is using it now and the pool lights stay on all night."

I suggested, "Perhaps others here who have not yet been baptized in the name of Christ would like to do that this evening."

We all trooped to the poolside. Although I would have liked to baptize the Jewish brother myself, I asked others who knew him better to perform the ceremony. Two people went into the pool, dressed as they were, and others joined them. Altogether six or more men and women were baptized that night. With great joy we adjourned back to the house.

I have to admit I was curious to know how a Jewish man could get a job in Saudi Arabia. But somehow he had been employed by an American company, and God used these unusual circumstances to open his heart and draw him to Jesus Christ.

In my travels all over Arabia, it seemed evident that Americans in particular were unafraid to declare that they were Christians. They were even willing to take risks to get the Word of God into the whole region. I often wished that other nationalities would show the same desire and boldness.

Years later, flying into that same country in November 1995 with Arabic Scriptures to distribute, I decided the greatest possibility for success lay in travelling via Dhahram rather than the capital city of Riyadh. Dhahram is an amazing city with wealthy homes and giant office buildings and shopping malls built after the discovery of oil. Expatriates were allowed to have a meeting place inside a compound, and the believers welcomed me.

I wanted to take 30 kilos of Bibles to Riyadh. Getting there by road I would have to pass through six checkpoints, which could be a problem. By plane I faced only one checkpoint.

Officials caught me with the literature before boarding the aircraft but allowed me on the flight, intending to inform Riyadh that I would be arriving. When I landed, security people confiscated the Arabic Bibles and allowed me to stay one night in a hotel. Then I was taken for many intense hours of interrogation before eight *mutawa* (religious police) as well as security and customs officers. Some of my stock had been placed right in front of everyone, on the floor. Eight of the men sat in a semi-circle behind me. Everyone took copies of the Scriptures, and while I was being questioned I could overhear a conversation going on between the men.

"Listen, Ahmed! 'I am the resurrection and the life. He who believes in me will never perish.'"

"Where does it say that?"

I thought, *Praise the Lord! They're having a Bible study!* But my interrogators were not happy and wanted me to sign a statement in Arabic.

"I cannot read this," I protested. "How can I sign it?"

They insisted that I sign or I'd be kept in prison, so I signed reluctantly, considering that I'd be of more use free than behind bars.

The officials had also assembled all the customs men who were on duty when I arrived. I was instructed to look through a one-way window and identify the one who had let me through.

I said I couldn't. They all had black beards and they all looked alike to me.

"Choose any of them!" they said.

"I can't do that. My God is a holy God. If I chose an innocent man and he was put in prison, God would judge me."

The officials were very angry and took me back to the hotel. The next day I was put into a car; two other vehicles drove in front and behind. I was taken to see a customs official who told me that I had brought an illegal consignment of Bibles. Then our motorcade drove out of the city into the desert. I thought of Edna and wondered, *Lord, is this it?*

Suddenly we arrived at a pair of great gates. They opened before us and we followed a driveway through beautiful grounds that led to a magnificent palace. The cars stopped; we got out and entered a luxurious *majlis*, an Arabic-style room with perhaps twenty-eight men sitting on embroidered floor cushions lining the walls, and low coffee tables. I was conducted further into a huge office and all the men in the *majlis* crowded in after me. A dignified-looking person who sat behind a large desk told me to sit down. A *mullah* (Muslim priest) sat opposite me in another chair.

The man behind the desk, obviously some kind of senior official, observed, "Mr Thomas, you are getting on in years."

"Yes," I acknowledged. "I'm a grandfather."

"You have grandchildren, and you do these things?"

"Yes, sir, because there are many who have never yet read the Injil, the Torah, and Zabur."

The official suddenly addressed the others in the room, who were mostly customs and immigration men along with some religious police from the mosque. "Why are you here? There's no need for you to be here."

He dismissed everyone so that only he, the *mullah*, and myself remained. We had a lovely talk, and he ended up warning me to be careful. He then spoke to the *mullah* at length, in Arabic. Finally he announced that all was well and handed me my passport.

"I like you, Mr Thomas, because you did not smuggle. You came openly to give these books as gifts."

He paused, then asked, "Where are you from, Mr Thomas?"

When I told him the town of Reading, in England, he enquired if I had been to the night club there or in other places he named. It was obvious that he had visited them. I told him that I didn't go to clubs.

At this point the *mullah* came and shook my hand and left the office.

"Where else in my country would you like to visit?" my examiner wanted to know.

"Jeddah," I told him.

"Go, and enjoy yourself."

"Can I bring Bibles with me?" Of course this was pushing my luck, and he shook his head.

"No."

As I was leaving the man asked if I would come and see him again, the next time I visited. Regretfully, this never happened for the reason I recount next. I did reach Jeddah, however, and had an interesting time. One special contact was with an Arab pilot who said the safest place for us to talk and pray was inside an aircraft simulator machine, in which we spent a total of twenty-five minutes. The Holy Spirit is just as real in a space like that as He is among a meeting of sincere intercessors.

* * *

My return to Saudi Arabia a year later was occasioned by an invitation from the British ambassador. He was planning to put on a private dinner at the embassy and wanted to give me the opportunity to speak. I would be staying at the embassy as his guest, so that I could also meet with other interested friends for several days. When I flew to Riyadh and presented my passport and visa at immigration, however, officials arrested me on the spot and told me I would be deported.

For the next sixteen hours I sat waiting for whatever would happen next. Meanwhile a diplomat was waiting outside the airport, trying to find out what had happened to me. God made wonderful use of that time while I was detained, because other people gravitated to me to ask questions. I was the only Westerner among many nationalities and had an open door to share about Jesus and the cross. The authorities inspected every inch of my luggage and found nothing. They deported me anyway and I returned to Edna in Cyprus.

Thirty-six hours after my arrest, one of my colleagues working with the underground church was arrested and confined in prison for two weeks. He was then transferred out of solitary to a cell with another man, a plant who endeavoured to extract information. After a month he was released.

* * *

Saudi Arabia and the United Arab Emirates allow millions of foreign workers into their countries to do the jobs that nationals are unwilling to perform. However, some minorities like Filipinos, Pakistanis, Indians, Bangladeshis, and Sri Lankans are treated with contempt, even those who are Muslims. In Abu Dhabi, several organizations including Christian churches work together to supply food, clothes, and other aid to migrant labourers and their families who have been left stranded by their employers.

I once met a Pakistani follower of Christ who told me he had asked his Arab sponsor if he could work only part time, from 7 a.m. to 1 p.m. When his boss asked him why, he told him honestly that he wanted to serve his Lord and speak to people about Jesus.

Amazingly, the boss agreed and reduced his salary to £170 a month. His rent was £70 a month and he had to support his wife and four children. Yet he had just spent the last seven and a half months working only part time and using the rest of the day to share the gospel at building construction sites and prisons. He had a great vision to reach the lost although he could not afford to purchase any Scriptures. I was glad that we were able to supply him with a good quantity of Arabic, Urdu, and other language literature, and friends donated a month's rent to further encourage this man's initiative.

Before I was made *persona non grata* from Saudi, I visited a secret meeting in an isolated place, miles from the nearest town. The journey was not easy but it proved well worth attending. The large room I entered was mostly in darkness except for one light bulb dangling from the ceiling in the centre. I was directed to stand under the light, lead in prayer, read from the Bible, and speak. Somewhere in the shadows someone interpreted. The only faces I could see belonged to those who were around my feet, yet I could sense the presence of many others in the darkness. I shared from the Book of Acts and how the early church was a persecuted church, but a continually praying church. Some Christians were imprisoned and others put to death but the message spread and the church grew into vast numbers.

I shared some up-to-date testimonies of others I knew who had come out of Islam and into the salvation and joy of knowing Jesus Christ, baptized and filled with the Holy Spirit. I could tell these stories encouraged the people present for they made excited exclamations and cried "Amen!"

It was a long meeting in very humid conditions and a long way back to a friend's house for a shower and rest afterwards. But I have often thought of the believers who were there, wondering how they fared and where they are now. I look forward to meeting them again one day in the light of heaven.

11
THROUGH GATES OF BRASS

Will God really step in to intervene for us when we are confronted by situations beyond our control? Before Edna and I embarked on our "mission impossible" to the Arab world, our Father promised He would break down gates of brass and cut through iron bars whenever they stood in the way of His work. And that's what we saw happen again and again – especially when it came to getting God's Word through airport customs! We were faced with opportunities that were brilliantly disguised by the enemy as impossibilities.

On one occasion when workers in a particular conservative country learned that we were both about to make a visit, they contacted us to say they were seriously in need of large quantities of Scriptures. We decided to oblige them by carrying in 200 kilos.

After arriving at our destination airport we picked up our boxes of books from the luggage belt and I said to Edna, "We'll put a hundred kilos in Arabic on your trolley, and a hundred on mine."

I loaded both trolleys and then said, "See that customs official over there? If he points to the right when you approach it means you have to go through the scanner. If he points to the left you're home free! Arabs like Western women, so give him a beautiful smile. Even if I get caught he'll let you through!"

"You're not hiding behind my skirts, are you?" Edna couldn't resist teasing.

She went ahead and greeted the official with a "*Salaam Alaikum*" and bright smile on her face. He looked at her and pointed right, to the scanner. I thought, *O Lord, please get me through!* But the official pointed right to me as well.

Each box contained 20 kilos of books. I started putting Edna's boxes onto the belt to be scanned, but she started pulling on my sleeve.

"I'm trying to be as quick as I can, darling!" I told her.

She whispered something and gestured so I looked up. The man who was supposed to be watching the screen was sound asleep, snoring.

We quickly pushed all our boxes through the scanner and snatched them on the other side, stacking them back on our trolleys. Just as we finished the man woke up.

Edna smiled again sweetly and asked, "Okay?"

He nodded.

That's what I'd call a case of divine sleeping sickness.

When we came out of the airport our contacts were waiting in their cars. Some of them were so excited to see us with the boxes that they forgot themselves and shouted, "Hallelujah!" and "Praise the Lord!"

Aware of police all around us, I tried to put a lid on their expressions of enthusiasm.

"Let's give glory to God when we're safely out of here!" I pleaded.

And that's exactly what we did.

* * *

Another time, after my boxes of books were confiscated at one particular Gulf airport, I set out for the Sharia court (not in the same country as the one described in an earlier chapter), to appeal for their release. The president of the court refused.

"You can take them back to Lebanon or Cyprus or wherever they are from," he instructed.

I objected that I couldn't do that because I couldn't pay the excess baggage charge of almost $1,000. "However," I added, "I know you won't destroy them, because they're the holy books of God."

The president was clearly frustrated. "All right. I will pay, and I will send them back!"

"Do you promise this in the name of God?"

"In the name of God I will do it."

He took my address.

As I emerged from the court a young man driving an expensive racing car stopped to pick me up, offering to take me to wherever I was staying. I got in thankfully and remarked, "This looks like a James Bond car. Does it fire bullets?"

"It *is* like a Bond car," he smiled. "What were you doing in Sharia court?"

I explained and he looked incredulous. "You brought the Bible here?"

The young man told me he was married and his family wanted him to take a second wife. "What would you say about that, as a Christian?"

I got my Bible out and read some verses in Ephesians about marriage and having one wife, and he said, "That's lovely. Read that again."

He was glad to accept a copy of the Injil and drove me to the door of the home where I was staying. Then he opened the boot and presented me with a model of his car, to give to the son of my host, along with a poster. I later found out from them that he was the racing champion of the whole Gulf region.

When I got back to Cyprus and shared what had happened in the Sharia court with my Christian friends, they were sceptical.

"That president will never send your Bibles back," they predicted.

Four days later I got a call from the airport. "Mr Tom, there's a lot of boxes here, waiting for you to pick up."

The president had kept his word. All the books were returned except for three copies. My friends were stunned, and together we gave thanks to the Lord. Then I looked at Edna.

"Edna, the Lord has told me something."

"I know what it is," she smiled. "You're to get on another flight and take those Bibles back."

So I took those books, added a few more, and off I went. Since God had told me to do it, He would get me through.

And He did. At customs an official welcomed me, using the affectionate term between beloved friends, "*habibi*". There was no problem and the "seeds" were delivered this time – all praise to our wonderful, triune God.

* * *

Once I was asked to take about a dozen masters of Christian videos into a conservative country. Normally I didn't take videos, only Scriptures, but because the need was great and opportunities for circulating them good, I agreed. As I went through the scanner at the destination airport they were detected in my boxes of books. Later I found out that another person was immediately deported for bringing in just two videos. However, the officials were so interested in these they let the Bible boxes go through! They kept the tapes and said I could have a receipt and claim them back from the ministry of censorship in three months.

Of course I didn't stay in that country, but a friend went to the ministry with my receipt after three months elapsed, and asked about the videos. He was told to return in another week's time. When he did he was invited for coffee by the minister and following twenty minutes or so of conversation my friend was asked what he wanted.

"The Christian videos that belonged to my friend," he said. The minister showed him into an office and there they were, officially stamped and ready for him to take away. The minister said, "They are very good videos." Those videos were copied and circulated widely, blessing and inspiring untold numbers of viewers.

* * *

When Saddam Hussein's army rolled into Kuwait in August 1990, thousands of residents of different nationalities fled into Jordan for asylum. Camps were set up outside the cities, which gave OM opportunities to help the people with medical and other practical needs. The team also ministered to the distressed emotional state of these refugees, sharing the gospel with them and distributing New Testaments in many languages.

Manara ("Lighthouse") Christian Bookshop in Amman

was magnificent and did everything possible to assist the OM team. The staff even prepared food to feed hundreds of displaced men, women, and children, which the team daily transported to the camps by lorry.

I had prepared a big consignment of over 200 kilos of Scriptures as well as children's Bible storybooks to send from Cyprus. An airline would carry these on the same flight that I was taking.

Just an hour before I was due to leave home, however, the phone rang and a voice said, "Tom, don't bring any special books with you today because there are difficulties at the airport."

I knew instantly what this meant but replied, "Too late. They are already on the aircraft, so pray me through when I get there."

As I'd been warned, the climate at the Amman airport was not encouraging. I approached customs with my books and spoke politely, explaining that I was working alongside Manara Ministries to help the refugees. I added that Jordan's king and government were doing a great work of compassion. The customs people smiled and responded, "*Shukran* (thank you). Go through."

A small miracle, perhaps, but my heart was racing.

Day after long day in the several weeks that followed we went among the people in the camps, feeding them, comforting and assisting any way we could as well as sharing copies of God's Word. I entered one large tent in the Sudanese camp and realized too late that it was set apart for Muslims to pray. Many of the men inside greeted me in a friendly way, however, and we got into a good, long conversation about the value of prayer.

"Can Christians pray?" they were curious to know. I instantly knelt in the middle of the tent and prayed to my Abba Father. I then offered each man a copy of the Arabic-English dual translation New Testament. They all accepted a copy, and more discussion followed. Eventually I had to leave. As I rose a tall, dignified-looking man spoke up.

"Why don't you say a prayer before you leave?"

I very gladly complied, from my heart. I cannot remember exactly what I prayed but the men listened and thanked me sincerely, calling me *habibi*, or good friend.

The following day as I was going around to different tents, two security men intercepted me and ordered, "Open your bag." Seeing all the New Testaments and Bibles I carried they said, "You must come with us to the senior officer, for you cannot do this."

We arrived at a temporary office building. The man in charge looked very busy but he listened to the guards, inspected my precious books, and told me to sit down. He would have to ring the government office in Amman about this, he told me. Meanwhile he gave me a cool soft drink, for the office had no fans and it felt like an oven.

In spite of repeated attempts to call his superiors the man wasn't able to get through to Amman, however. He said he would wait awhile and try again. After three hours passed without any success the officer told me I could take my bag and go, but I must only bring food, not books, if I returned to the camp.

I went back to where I was staying in Amman, knelt down, and asked God for guidance. Opening my Bible I read from Nehemiah 6:11: "Should a man like me run away? Or should someone like me go into the temple to save his life? I will not go!" I knew I would be quite safe staying in Amman and sharing in fellowships and schools in that city, but what about all of those refugees who needed to hear?

So the next day I went back to the camps on the food lorry that was also carrying boxes of books. I prayed that not one Bible would be lost and that I could move freely among the refugees. When the people spotted me at the gate they shouted, "Injil man! Have you got any more Injils?" I said yes rather quietly, because the same two security men were there, watching. I acted unconcerned, however, and they spoke to each other and smiled at me. I am convinced they thought I had obtained permission, so they made no objection. In fact, a few days later they approached me and asked, "Have you any more Injils left in your bag?"

I showed them that I had only a few, and to my delight they asked for copies for themselves. God was in it all.

* * *

In an earlier chapter I related how we were able to distribute large quantities of Arabic Bibles in Kuwait, after the defeat of Saddam Hussein's army. We ran out of Scriptures all too soon and when I got back to Cyprus I was eager to return to Kuwait City to take advantage of the glorious, wide-open door. But the next time I landed everything was different. The country had got itself organized, and so had the airport system. When I landed and presented my passport and visa at customs and immigration I was greeted with, "Oh, yes, Mr Thomas. You've been here before, haven't you? We know all about you."

"Of course," I responded lightly. "I'm an open book."

"Mr Thomas – sit over there on that seat," the official directed unsmilingly.

I sat for about forty minutes on a metal chair and then there was a change of staff. I told the officer that the previous man still had my passport. He told me to sit down again. I sat in that chair for three days and three nights. I couldn't call anyone and no one approached me except to escort me to a toilet and allow me to buy a bottle of water.

I felt that they were trying to break me. There were times when the devil urged me, "Go on, show them who you are! You're British, a child of God. Be bold!"

But then I heard the Spirit say, "Be patient. Wait. I promised you that I would open bars of iron."

Of course, the person who was to meet me outside the airport caught on that something was wrong. He sent a pre-arranged message to Edna, back in Cyprus: *The farmer arrived with seeds but got stuck in mud.*

Edna immediately alerted a prayer chain and everyone on it began intensive intercession for me.

At long last I was called to a desk.

"Seven days, then you go!" the officer barked.

Vastly relieved that I wasn't being immediately deported, even though I couldn't stay the month that I'd anticipated, I took my passport and went in search of my boxes that had been sitting, abandoned, in the baggage area. The customs officers there wanted to know where I had been for three days and I explained. Now, I said, I needed to find my precious books. God melted their hearts. Not only did they help me find and load my boxes without inspecting their contents, they pushed the heavy trolleys out of the airport themselves and got me a taxi!

I believe that if I hadn't waited all that time to pick up those boxes, they would have been opened and confiscated and I'd have lost everything. God did a miracle through that delay – but it was the biggest test of patience I ever endured!

* * *

At one point I had to send my passport to the British High Commission in Cyprus since I was running out of pages. I also had a few "*persona non gratas*" stamped in it, so I needed a new passport. The High Commission sent back my old passport with the new one attached to it by a rather impressive seal. I didn't really want to carry both of them but I needed to leave on another trip right away.

The country I was visiting had no Christian churches so I had brought along a couple hundred kilos of books and a few copies of the *Jesus* film. At immigration they just stamped the new passport without looking at the old one. But at customs the officials ordered me to open one of my boxes. I did so, telling them it contained the holy books of God.

"Oh no, no no!" they cried in alarm. Then they spotted the films and exclaimed, "Video? No videos!"

They asked to see my passport and when I handed it over, they were startled by the official-looking seal that attached the old and new passports together.

"Diplomat!" they murmured together, exchanging glances. "*Diplomat.* You may go through."

Little did the High Commission realize the favour they had done in attaching that seal!

Entering Yemen after another very long trip and feeling exhausted, all my luggage was screened and marked for examination. Two unpleasant customs men were just beginning their task when an Arab man nearby shouted, "Mr Thomas, remember me? I worked in the British Embassy as translator, and you often visited."

"Of course I remember you," I replied.

The customs men, listening to this exchange, reacted quickly by clearing my boxes. Nothing was opened – they too obviously thought I was a diplomat!

After another airport arrival some time later, however, the customs officers on duty decided to make a real meal of me. In the midst of their incriminations I caught sight of a well-dressed man who was just beyond the desk on the other side. Like my translator acquaintance above he was waving to get my attention and calling out to me.

"Mr Thomas! Hello, Mr Thomas!" he shouted loudly. "You remember me? We had coffee together at British Embassy!"

I racked my brains but this time couldn't remember ever meeting this man.

"You going to British Embassy?"

"Yes," I nodded, since it was my usual practice to check in at the embassy.

"Good. Maybe we have coffee again!" he yelled.

The listening customs officials also decided I must be a diplomat. They promptly waved me through.

I never saw my unknown "friend" again.

12
OF CAMELS AND CALAMITIES

T ravelling so many thousands of miles over the years in territory long claimed by our adversary the devil, one can expect a few hostile encounters and so-called accidents. But I remember the response God gave me the time a Muslim man snarled in my face and promised, "One day I will kill you."

"Will you?" I returned. "Well, let me tell you what you can do after you have killed me."

"What?"

"Nothing – for killing me is all you can do. Only the flesh dies; my spirit and soul go to Jesus and God."

The young man stared at me, speechless. He had no rebuttal.

I had a similar experience in Yemen. Six men came to see me with faces set and determined and they, too, declared their intention to kill me.

"You think you will be doing me a disservice, but in fact you will be doing me a favour," I told them, meeting their gaze. "You will be releasing my soul right into the presence of God the Father."

A week later the group came back. We were very busy at the time but I greeted them with the customary *Salaam Alaikum*. Unlike my last encounter with them, one man

189

returned a polite *Alaikum Salaam*. And this time when I offered him a copy of the Gospel, he accepted it.

Christians need have no fear, only the fear which comes from reverence for our all-powerful God, and a faith that pleases Him.

An American friend (whom I'll call Jack) and his wife had developed a great love for the Arab people and had been used by God to share the gospel with many in the southeastern corner country of the Arabian Peninsula, Oman. One time Jack and I made plans to visit a former British Air Force base to conduct a service in the chapel, which was still in use by a goodly number of civilian workers. Since he had just purchased a new car he offered to drive us to the base. However, just prior to leaving Salalah, something went wrong with the vehicle's mechanics and we were forced to take it back to the dealers. They were helpful, but since they could not immediately correct the problem they offered the loan of an old, well-worn Land Rover.

"It won't let you down," they promised. So Jack and I started across the desert towards the mountains. It was already dark and since the lights on the old vehicle were not very bright, Jack drove cautiously. All of a sudden a large camel loomed in the road in front of us.

Camels have been called "ships of the desert", with good reason. For thousands of years they have reliably transported goods and people across Arabian sands and played a vital role in the economy. The animals were and still are also used for entertainment, celebrations, and competitions, especially by the desert-dwelling Bedouins who regard them with affection. Camel racing is a very popular sport; winners can be sold for huge amounts of money.

Although Jack tried his best to avoid the obstacle in our path, it was too late. We hit the camel, which rolled over the top of the Land Rover and fell dead. Most of the animal's weight impacted my side. The roof was crushed, and glass showered onto my head and face.

We were actually very fortunate. It isn't uncommon in this part of the world for drivers or passengers to be killed by collisions with stray camels. Jack did all he could to help me but there was a lot of blood and he was afraid I was badly injured. Just then, from what seemed like nowhere, a group of Omani soldiers appeared. It turned out that the men were from a tented camp in the desert. They immediately rushed me to a first aid tent while Jack was taken to the police to explain what had happened.

The doctor who attended me was from India but he had just completed six years' training in the UK. He patiently extracted the glass fragments from my head, perceiving from my glazed expression that I was in shock. As he was finishing up and administering some medication, the police arrived.

"Get off that trolley and come with us," they ordered abruptly. I was to report immediately to the local police station, wherever that was.

The doctor protested that his patient needed to rest for the night. He would personally escort me to the station in the morning. They refused this suggestion, however, so dizzy as I was I started to get dressed, with help from the doctor. While we were doing this he slipped a piece of paper into my hand.

"You will need that," he told me. I thought it was a prescription and put it in my pocket.

The police drove me to the station, where I was delighted

to be reunited with Jack. He was clearly perturbed, however, and shared that the authorities seemed to think we had been drinking alcohol. Furthermore, the owner of the camel had been contacted and would be arriving at dawn to lay a claim for its value.

I then took the doctor's signed note from my pocket. "No alcohol in the blood," I read. Those words saved us from what could have been an unpleasant residential stay in prison.

We were allowed to sleep overnight on wooden benches. Although we managed an hour or two we were both exhausted by the time early dawn arrived, along with the camel owner. The police announced that we were liable for an amount equivalent to a thousand British pounds ($1,500).

Fortunately we were able to contact friends in Muscat, in the north of Oman, to ask if they could somehow raise the money for us. But then we received another shock when the camel owner started shouting at us. I guessed that he was demanding more money, but not knowing Arabic fluently I couldn't make out why he was so annoyed. It had been an accident, after all.

It turned out that the camel we killed was pregnant. More money therefore had to be negotiated to cover the added loss. Eventually, with the wonderful help of Christians in Oman, the man received his compensation money and we were released. I have to applaud Jack for his wise and gracious interaction with the Omani authorities, earning their mutual respect. He, with his charming wife, did a great ministry in Oman and elsewhere.

A very different sort of accident occurred in 1999, in the Gulf sheikhdom of Ras Al Khaimah. Dennis Gurney was an Anglican evangelical priest who had worked faithfully for a number of years in the United Arab Emirates and established several small Christian fellowship centres. He had persevered in asking the very conservative sheikh of Ras Al Khaimah (RAK), for legal permission to have a worship centre for Christians, which was finally granted. RAK was called the Cinderella of the seven emirates because it was far less developed than the modern city of Dubai, two hours' drive away.

We had known Dennis and his wife for over a dozen years when he invited Edna and me to spend six months expanding the fledgling work he had started in the sheikhdom. He also wanted us to live in a small villa as a chaplain's house. My friend was a marvel of enthusiasm who always seemed to squeeze forty-eight hours of activity into a twenty-four hour day. In fact we were much alike, and sometimes when you get two visionaries together you don't always see the other brother's vision the same way as you see your own!

We agreed more than we disagreed, however, and worked with the same heart and aim: to spread God's good news in as many languages as possible. So Edna and I moved into a rented property in Ras Al Khaimah. Our meeting place was in the grounds of a run-down building that had once been a sports club. Dennis had purchased a portacabin which was air-conditioned and could hold up to a hundred and fifty or more people. We held services in English, Arabic, a few Indian dialects, Tagalog for Filipinos, and other language groups, supplying many Scriptures for them all. Since a variety of international families worked in RAK, children's Bibles and books were also much in demand.

Although we were not permitted to advertise the church or place a cross on the building, we experienced much blessing and rejoiced over the growth of the different congregations that used the facilities. On one very hot Friday afternoon I told Edna that I was going over to the centre to make sure all was ready for the evening service. Friday is commonly observed as a holy day throughout the Muslim world, so most Christian workers are also free to meet together on that day to worship. I wanted to check that the air conditioning was on and that the water in the washrooms and toilets was working.

"I'm coming with you," said Edna.

"No need," I told her. "Stay here in the cool of house. It's 46°C out there and you know you have problems when it's too hot. Just leave it to me."

Edna is a wonderful wife and we have enjoyed a long and loving marriage. She generally agrees with my decisions, but on this occasion she insisted on accompanying me. How thankful I am that she did!

We arrived inside the walled church compound. It was blisteringly hot. I checked the air conditioners and all was well. The new motor pump I had installed to fill the water tank was working away nicely... except that it was not pumping water!

I told Edna that I needed to climb the ladder up to the tank, which was 24 feet above the ground, because the automatic valve had probably stuck.

"Oh, Tom darling, don't go up that high!" she exclaimed.

But there was no other way; all the toilets and sinks had no water. The folks would soon be arriving for the evening service. So up I went.

I had just climbed onto the tank and opened the lid when suddenly the structure moved and I was thrown off, falling all the way down to the concrete base below. I had paid workers to bolt the tank down, but they had decided the weight of the water would be sufficient to hold it in place.

It was a near-miracle that I wasn't killed. Edna raised the alarm and a boy on a bicycle raced 300 yards to the main road and stopped a land cruiser with an Arab driver. Nearby stood six Filipino Christians who had been waiting twenty minutes for a taxi. Three of them were nurses. They all rushed to help and the Arab driver, a wonderful gentleman, got me to the hospital.

On duty was a Christian Egyptian surgeon who quickly called his medical team together and went to work. Unlike Humpty Dumpty who couldn't be put together again by all the king's horses or all the king's men, the "King's man" was able to put me together again. I sustained a total of twenty-four fractures, including two broken wrists, fingers, left arm, and several ribs. A gash in my forehead required twelve stitches. (I joked to the hospital staff that having my head opened allowed more light in!) The surgeon at this hospital said my hands and wrists were a mess; I would need to have extensive surgery.

Through God's goodness two close friends, Dennis and Marleen Turner, were visiting us from Bahrain for the weekend. They stayed with Edna and me before I went into the operating theatre, sharing Scripture verses of encouragement and assuring me that they would be praying for me throughout the surgery. They also took Edna to the police station to make a statement. The police went to check out the scene of the accident and expressed wonder that I had survived. "Did someone push him?" was one of their questions. Another – "Was he trying to kill himself?"

Messages flooded into our OM office from around the world. International leader George Verwer rang from a train in Germany; other dear friends phoned and faxed from New Zealand, Australia, Singapore, USA, Canada, and all over Europe and the Middle East, assuring us of their love and prayers. Of course scores of local friends also visited each day.

I was the only non-Muslim and non-Arab patient in the hospital, but it seemed that all the staff and daily visitors had heard about the "Christian *imam*" who fell from such a great height and lived. Everyone was wonderfully kind. The consultant, surgeons, sisters, and nurses kept repeating, "Pastor Tom, you are a miracle." Christian Filipina nurses surrounded my bed each morning at 7:20 to pray for me. Even the cleaners came to my room to affirm, "God has been good to you!" Any hopes we had entertained of keeping a low profile were blown away.

As I lay helplessly with my arms in plaster, elevated into the air, I was treated every morning at five to the call to prayer. After several times of listening to the Arabic chanting echo through the wards for twenty minutes I decided, I am a Christian. Why shouldn't I also be allowed a time of worship? So as loudly as I could I sang out "The Lord's Prayer" and followed that up with "This is the Day" and "Morning Has Broken". Then I went on to pray aloud and quote Scriptures.

Astonishingly enough, I wasn't barred from this expression of worship in the ward. In fact, all during the day patients in wheelchairs rolled over to me to ask, "Is that how Christians pray?" They marvelled. They had no idea that Christians enjoyed prayer and times of devotion. I did a lot of Scripture distribution from my bedside table. In fact, Edna had to replenish my literature stock every day and even *Jesus* videos went out. The results were gratifying.

One Arab gentleman, a high official in the Gulf region, was paralysed from the waist down. He came daily to my bedside in his wheelchair, talking about what he was reading in the Injil and asking sincere questions, seeking answers. After I left the hospital he rang me regularly with more questions, and said my answers brought him inner peace.

Edna was my constant help all through the long hospital confinement and longer recuperation at home. In spite of the indignity of not being able to help myself for months, I was blessed with the most positive nurse anyone could find in the Gulf. She learned to drive the car there for the first time, and did not once scold me or remind me that she had warned me not to climb the tower.

One day she observed, "Tom darling, you do need your hair cut, it's very straggly. Let's go into town and find a barber shop."

My two arms were still in slings but we duly found a shop, and upon entering it we noticed a small Filipino boy was sitting in the barber chair. His dad and mum stood close beside him; perhaps it was his very first haircut.

As we sat down to await my turn, the boy's mother said to me, "You are Pastor Tom, yes?"

I replied in the affirmative and introduced Edna.

"Pastor Tom, on the day of your accident and admittance to the hospital, I was duty sister in the operating theatre."

I thanked her for being there and said how grateful I was

to all the hospital staff for helping me and serving me so graciously.

She asked, "Did you know that you spoke to the surgeons after being sedated, and during your operation? We were amazed."

This came as a surprise to me, to say the least. "Did I say something silly or sensible?" I was curious to know.

"Well, after the two surgeons sedated you they told you they had to cut the wedding ring off your finger and also cut through your socks because your hands and feet were swelling so fast.

"With your eyes closed, you said to them: 'Do you gentlemen know what Jesus did for His disciples before His arrest and crucifixion?'

"They answered 'no', so then you told them Jesus washed their feet and taught them a lesson of humility in how to serve one another...' You said more until you finally went under the anaesthesia. The surgeons were astonished and one exclaimed, 'We have not had a patient like this man before, have we?'

"The other surgeon agreed. He was an Egyptian Orthodox Christian, the other man a strict Muslim. But even while they were operating on you, you said 'Jesus... Jesus' several times, and the doctors looked at each other in wonder."

The little boy's haircut was now finished. The couple shook Edna's hand, touched my arm, and bid us farewell. The Indian barber was also looking quite moved by what he had heard.

I have often, since then, thought of those two surgeons. I also remember Dennis and Marleen, who helped us so much and could write their own book about serving as couriers and sowers of God's Word in Arabia. Although most of the world knows little or nothing about them, the Turners sowed thousands of precious seeds throughout the nations of the Gulf, even getting large consignments into Saudi Arabia for the underground believers in Christ. Edna and I honour them, and we have often raised our voices to the throne of God in thanksgiving for them: ordinary folks who did an extraordinary ministry.

Later, during the weeks that I was laid up in plaster at home in Ras Al Khaimah, a local Muslim priest (*imam*) came to visit with one of his elders. I was resting in the front room when Edna answered the front door. I heard her say, "Please come in," and wondered who it could be.

The two men walked in and I thanked them for coming to see me. They sat down and the elder, without asking, instantly picked up an Arabic New Testament that I always kept on the coffee table. From then on he took no part in the conversation; he was transfixed by what he was reading.

Edna and I were the only expatriates in the area at that time and we lived among the people without modern conveniences, like air conditioning. The *imam* said politely that he had heard from the hospital and many in the mosque that I had had a terrible accident, and said it was his duty to call and ask if there was anything he could do. I responded that his visit was much appreciated.

We talked about the church and then the *imam* commented, "You probably hear our prayers from the mosque five times a day. You Christians don't pray five times a day."

"No," I agreed, "we don't. We pray more than that."

"*What?* I don't see you going to church that often."

"That's correct. We don't have to be in church. As followers of Christ and having a personal relationship with Him and our Father God, we pray when we are walking, running, lying down or getting up; or whether we are driving a car, travelling in an aeroplane or train or bus. We have continual access into the holy presence of God and I can 'breathe' prayers to my Abba Father wherever I am, wherever I go."

"I have never heard of 'breathing' prayers," he said in a serious, enquiring tone. "So this is what you do daily? How do you do it?"

I demonstrated by praying aloud the Lord's Prayer, thankful for the marvellous opportunity.

"Where did you get that prayer?" asked the priest.

"Jesus gave it to us."

"Are there many Christians like you?" he wanted to know.

"Oh yes, there are millions of us."

We went on to the subject of fasting.

"You Christians do not fast," my visitor asserted.

"Oh yes, we do. You Muslims don't truly fast. During the month of Ramadan you don't eat during the day, but you eat all night. [More food is actually consumed during Ramadan than any other time of year!] So it's actually a farce, not a fast. We Christians eat no food while we fast, and drink only water."

"For how long?"

"We can do it for one day, several days or several weeks at a time."

"That is in your Book? And you don't eat? How do you go about it?" he demanded.

"We must be careful not to let others know when we are fasting and praying. The Lord Jesus tells us that we are to look normal and cheerful. It is an act between us and God. Speaking to Him in secret, He rewards us openly. That is true fasting."

The man was utterly amazed. Like most Muslims, he was completely unaware that Christians fast.

He looked over at the elder, who was still totally absorbed in reading the New Testament, and said something in Arabic. The elder immediately put the Book down and stood up. I told the *imam* that his elder was welcome to have the copy, and he was welcome to one also.

He did not reply to that, spoke again in Arabic to the elder, and then turned to thank me for our conversation.

"See you again," he said with a smile, then let himself and his companion out. He did not return, but he always raised his arm when seeing me from a distance. He always seemed to be in a hurry. Edna and I prayed for the man and his family; his elder, too, and thanked God for the encounter.

When we finally got to England months later, my arms still in slings, a consultant took X-rays and stated, "Mr Hamblin, you are a complicated mess!"

Edna chuckled. "I've been saying that for years!"

We were both most grateful when two bone graft operations from hip to wrist on both sides finally ended the continuous pain, and physiotherapy gradually restored strength to my hands and fingers. Although the cost of surgery seemed enormous, God moved his international family to send gifts to help. Even the CanOxy oil company that knew us in Aden, with many of its employees attending the church, took up a generous collection among the staff. All of my medical fees were covered. Once again our wise and all-loving Father had taught us that this whole painful "accident" – not something we would have chosen to include in our journey of faith – could be used to accomplish far more than we dreamed possible.

As the psalmist put it, "I will not die but live, and will proclaim what the Lord has done."[9]

9 Psalm 118:17

13

DIAMONDS IN THE DARKNESS

I love Muslims, but my heart aches at the darkness that Islam has brought to so many millions. They are men and women just like you and me, except that they have been born into a system that grips every aspect of their lives. Islam is religious and it is political, but it is not spiritual because it teaches that it is blasphemy to say that God is your Father, that it is impossible to have fellowship with Him.

But we should understand that Muslims in the Middle East are approachable. They are not all fanatics or terrorists, as some believe. They are very hospitable and it is easy to make friends. They are also reachable with the gospel. *Redeemable.* Tens of thousands of Muslims are disillusioned with Islam, and God's Spirit is at work to open their hearts to the message of Christ.

Once these men and women become His, there is no stopping them. These are the treasures that God told Edna and me we could expect to find as we served Him: "I will give you hidden treasures, riches stored in secret places, so that you may know that I am the Lord, the God of Israel, who summons you by name" (Isaiah 45:3).

A poignant statement made by one suffering convert whom we knew for over nine years remains with me still: "When they first persecuted, arrested, and harmed me ten years ago it was hard to bear, Tom and Edna. But now when they take me away and hurt me I don't find it too difficult, for I know," he added with emphasis and a smile, "Jesus is right beside me."

Once I was invited to speak at an Anglican church in the Singapore that had a congregation of over one thousand. Afterwards the minister told me that he'd received an email from someone in Iran, asking for a Persian Bible.

"I don't know how he happened to write to me," he mused. "I don't know anyone in Iran."

I read the email and discovered that it came from a student. Taking the request back to Cyprus with me, I wrote back to the young man and offered to send a Bible if he would tell me how to do it safely.

He suggested that I declare it as a "book of history". I did this and he soon wrote back.

"It is so wonderful!" he exclaimed. "My friends and I have been reading the Bible four hours a day, and we have all become Christians. Please, can you send me six more copies?"

I gladly packed the copies and sent them, but they never reached the student. So he gave me three individual addresses and pleaded with me to send a Bible to each of them. These arrived safely, and we later learned that a group was meeting regularly for study.

* * *

I once travelled to a mountain village in Lebanon with a few bags of Scriptures, and met up with an old Arab who had only two teeth. He gave me a big gummy smile.

"*Salaam Alaikum!*"

"*Alaikum Salaam*," I returned, and we shook hands. Then he placed a finger on my heart and questioned, "Isa?"

"Oh yes! I know Jesus," I smiled warmly at the old man.

He then removed his finger and placed it over his own heart. "Isa," he repeated, and made the sign of the cross.

How was it that this soul who was seemingly illiterate and living in such a remote village, could also testify to having Jesus in his heart? How had he come to faith?

I put my hand into my bag and produced an Injil in Arabic, offering it to him. He began to cry then, throwing his arms around me and kissing me many times. (In the Middle East it's the men who do the kissing, I'd discovered. I'd never been kissed so many times in all my life!)

We both wept, for I sensed this was the first time this man had ever held in his hands a copy of God's Word, in his own language. The Lord had brought us together in a unique way.

In our travels, Edna and I have found many people who have never had a copy of the Bible, never read a single verse or had the gospel explained to them; but they have seen Jesus in dreams or visions.

People say to me, "Tom, do you mean people actually come to Jesus in a dream or vision?" I say that in His grace, Jesus appears to them. Our Sovereign Lord then arranges it so that someone eventually meets them and helps them find the way, the truth, and the life. It is interesting that when His Word actually gets into their hands, they no longer have such dreams. They have the Word of God to read for themselves.

"I revealed myself to those who did not ask for me; I was found by those who did not seek me," the Lord says in

Isaiah 65:1. "To a nation that did not call on my name, I said, 'Here am I, here am I.'"

* * *

I heard of one occasion when a group of Orthodox Christians were together worshipping, burning incense and chanting prayers, when the police burst in upon them. The officers did not harm or arrest the church members but destroyed the icons and crucifix.

The leader protested, "Why are you doing this? Those pictures mean a lot to us."

The senior officer responded, "Why? Because the image you have of Jesus is not the Lord Jesus who I have seen in my dreams."

We received a letter from a man named Achmed that reaffirms how our loving God persists in wooing those who don't know Him.

"I grew up as a devout Muslim," he wrote, "nurtured in the holy Quran for twenty-four years. After graduating from the University of Medina I became a lecturer.

"It was in Mecca, in 1989, that the Lord appeared to me in a vision. I saw a dried-up tree a short distance away and heard a voice saying, 'Where you are there is no life.'

"I was confused by this and went away to start searching the Quran and the hadiths, sayings and proverbs of the Prophet Muhammad. I found a verse where God speaks of Jesus, and many other references to Isa. Every time I opened the Quran it spoke of Him! I began to realize that God was saying to me, this is where life is. In Jesus.

"My eyes were opened. I saw that I had been in darkness since birth so I prayed, 'Show me the way,' and He did. I called my family and friends together and shared the truth that had been revealed to me.

"They were angry, threatened me, and called *mullahs* to argue with me, but the priests were confused and defeated when I shared about my search. Finally one of the *mullahs* stood and said that whoever took my life would be rewarded by Allah, because I had become an apostate."

Achmed was forced to flee for his life. In the country where he took refuge he saw a building with a cross on it. He went inside and learned that it was a Roman Catholic Church. The priest showed him Scriptures, and Achmed confessed his sins and asked Jesus to become his Saviour. But he was disturbed by the images he saw around the church. He had worshipped images in Mecca like the Black Stone, the cornerstone of the Kaaba. Muslims also venerated saints and the graves of the holy ones. He left the church and went across the street to get some coffee at a café.

"While I was there," he recounted, "a group of people came in wearing T-shirts that said 'Good News Messengers'. One man started talking with me and I discovered that he was a converted Muslim scholar! He encouraged me and instructed me in my newfound faith. God is now calling me to preach the gospel in the power of the Holy Spirit. I am an ambassador for Christ, not ordained by men. Christ is my King and my call is to the Muslims."

I think of another man whose name and country I cannot reveal, so we will call him Ali. At the time that he introduced himself to me, Ali was a married man with a family. He was also a secret believer. He told me that several years earlier his company had sent him to another country to teach technical matters to the staff there, in order to further the company's growth.

Ali was then a committed Muslim, but he found himself working among a Christian workforce which was very pleasant and friendly. They belonged to the Roman Catholic Church.

After a month, the staff invited Ali to attend the wedding celebration of a colleague at work. He accepted and went along. He had never before entered a Christian church and was surprised to see the priest dressed in robes with embroidered emblems, and the church smelling of sweet incense.

It was when the priest started to read from the Bible that he was gripped. The reading was from Ephesians 5:22–33, describing how a husband and wife should love each other "as Christ does the church".

After the service, during the reception, Ali spoke to the priest and asked questions about Christian marriage, and the portion of Scripture he had spoken about. The priest offered him a Bible which he gladly accepted. As Ali read the Gospels the light shone into his heart. He knelt down in the privacy of his own room and worshipped Jesus.

Ali was, as we often term it, born again. Heaven above did indeed seem to him "a deeper blue" and "earth around a sweeter green", as the hymn goes. The Holy Spirit filled him and he was later baptized secretly in the country of his birth. Upon returning to his family he shared what had happened with his wife. She was shocked and agitated. What if their neighbours discovered he was now a Christian? He would be killed and they would be without a provider. She would have to marry another man. His wife also worried about the children's reaction. What would happen if they told their friends that their father had become an infidel, an apostate?

After the children went to bed that night he read the New Testament to her. She, too, began to understand that this was the real truth of God as Abba Father, and Jesus His Son. She received Him as her Saviour. Now she and Ali rejoice that they are able to live on a spiritually higher plain, close to God's heart.

For the sake of safety I cannot give you the whole account of what transpired after that, except to say this couple endured opposition and tragedy. I will only add that Ali sought me out one day, wanting to know if I thought it would be wrong for him to go back to the mosque once a month, just to be seen by others. This would lessen the pressure that was being applied, he explained.

"But I will not be worshipping 'Allah' at all when I bow down in the mosque. My whole inner being will be worshipping Abba Father and Jesus my Saviour."

I drew Ali's attention to Naaman, the healed leper in the Scriptures who faced a similar problem and asked a man of God about it. The prophet had simply replied, "Go in peace."

Ali was very grateful for that reassurance.

* * *

We know two Christian Filipina girls who worked as nurses in a modern Arab hospital in one of the large cities. A lady in their care who had been severely ill and considered to be dying, slowly began to make progress. After about three weeks she was able to sit up and feed herself, and the nurses were delighted.

On the day before she was to be discharged the woman called the two girls to her bedside.

"I've been watching you two," she said. "You are Christians, aren't you?"

"Yes," they admitted readily. "We are."

"I know that. You love Jesus."

They smilingly agreed.

"When are you off duty? I will send a car for you. I want to give you a dinner with my family, to say thanks. You have already met some of them."

Sure enough, when the girls had their day off, a big black Mercedes came for them and they were driven to a huge, palatial home. They were conducted up to the third floor and saw that a great feast had been prepared, and the sons and wives and children were all waiting.

While the two girls ate, they could not help noticing the conversation between husbands and wives was relaxed and congenial, to a degree highly unusual in Arab families. After the meal the lady announced, "Come with us. We want to show you something."

The family took the girls downstairs to the floor underneath the house. Here was a large room with beautiful carpets, cushions and air-conditioning, without furniture except for a wooden table against the wall. On the table was a cross.

"We, too, are Christians," their hostess told them simply.

She added that the young women were welcome to visit their home again, but asked them not to speak to anyone about this room.

* * *

After Edna and I returned to Yemen in 1998, a pleasant, soft-spoken Yemeni man in Western clothes introduced himself to me.

"Do you remember me?" he asked.

I admitted that although his face was familiar, I didn't recognize his name.

"I can never forget you," he smiled. "In 1993 and 1994 you rode your bicycle around Aden with holy Injils in your bags. I often wanted to ask for one but I was afraid."

He related how he had, however, finally worked up his courage to come to me to ask the many questions he had about Jesus Christ. I now recalled that although he made it clear that he was a Muslim, married and with two small children, I had discerned that he was a genuine seeker. I felt sure at the time that he would ask me for a copy of the Injil. Instead he said, "I would like to request a copy of the Torah, Zabur, and Injil, please, and I will pay what you ask."

He wanted the whole Arabic Bible! I wrapped one in paper for his safety and put it into a plastic bag. He thanked me, shaking my hand with firmness and looking straight into my eyes. His countenance reflected great pleasure. The man explained that he had returned to see me a few months later and ask more questions, but I had left for Cyprus or some other destination.

"Those questions are no longer questions," he assured me, "for God has given me the answers to them by His Spirit."

My heart missed a beat or two. His demeanour was so full of light I guessed what his next words would be.

"You see, Mr Thomas, I am a Christian like you," he said, confirming my hope and sharing how he had made up his mind after listening to Christian Arabic broadcasts. "But I am a secret Christian. I cannot come to your church services or be seen too often coming to the clinic."

"I fully understand that difficulty," I assured him. "Perhaps we could meet somewhere else, late at night?"

He smiled again and said, "I will be okay. I have built an extra room in my house. It is my secret room where I read the Bible and worship God and His Son, my Saviour, and listen to the radio station."

He explained that his two children were still young and did not know of the existence of this room.

"But a time will come when I will tell them it is my study room and I need to be quiet there. My wife knows I am a Christian, and she is soon to become one as well!"

That was the last time we met, and Edna and I have prayed often for the safekeeping of this man and his wife.

I have had the privilege of baptizing many Muslim background believers. Just one of those people that comes to mind baptized six other individuals in the two years that followed his own immersion; he then led a group that met secretly to worship and study God's Word. Christ is building His church, and the gates of hell shall not prevail against it.[10]

Some people in the West have said to me, "But Tom, should they be secret believers? Surely they should come out into the open, nail their colours to the mast!"

I respond by referring them to John 19:38: "Joseph was a disciple of Jesus, but secretly because he feared the Jewish leaders."

"You see," I point out, "even then there were secret believers. Later Christians were forced to live in the Roman catacombs."

I am convinced there is a place for secret believers in Arabia and in many other parts of the world today. To

---

10 See Matthew 16:18

all who are reading this book, I would like to ask you to remember to pray for brothers and sisters who live as secret Christians: God's diamonds in dark places.

14
BRITAIN AND BEYOND

Edna and I made Cyprus our base until August 2001. Moving home to England after fifteen and a half years was more of a relocation than a retirement. We needed to spend some months sorting ourselves out, reintegrating into our local church and community, and spending quality time with our family.

By this time our daughter Sharon was very happily married to Stuart Mason, the fine Christian son of missionary parents. The two were very active in the same mission fellowship in which Edna and I were members for many years. They both had true servant hearts, and although they were not able to have children they accepted this as the will of God. Sadly, following twenty blessed years together, Stuart died suddenly at age forty-four. This was a loss for all the family for he was loved and esteemed by everyone who knew him.

Our son Mark was married to a lovely Christian and they had two beautiful girls. Sadly, however, the marriage bond broke. Mark has now remarried and he and Sue have two talented and active daughters. Edna and I can claim four granddaughters; the first two have given birth to boys, so we also have two great grandsons who are a joy to the whole family circle.

I remember once saying to my son when he blamed himself for the failure of his first marriage, "You have to live with the consequences of forgiven sin." We all do, if we are honest. Yet the grace of God continually rolls like a mighty ocean in its fullness. He knows us all through and through and He is not willing that any should perish, but that we should all come to repentance. This gracious Father of ours also loves restoration and re-creation, and imputes righteousness so that we can impart righteousness.

Even as Edna and I resettled in Britain, however, our priorities remained: raising funds for literature and projects in Muslim nations, and campaigning to raise awareness and involvement among Christians in the West.

As many readers will be aware, Islam is the fastest-growing religion in the United Kingdom as well as other parts of Europe. In Britain the country's Muslim population has nearly doubled in the past decade. And although we all like to assume we can all live in harmony, racism does exist. I am not a racist but I am a realist and I can foresee developments that will cause great grief in our land.

Perhaps it would be well to say something here about attitudes. We have met some missionaries to the Arabs who are anti-Jewish and strongly believe that the Jews of today are not part of God's future plans. We also know some Christians and missionaries who are anti-Arab, with little or no desire for their salvation, and so pro-Israel that they feel the Jews can do no wrong.

Is it possible for any of us to be "balanced believers"? Lord, help us to hear from you alone and do your will. Jesus put it so simply: "Follow *Me*." We need to be interested in all missionary activity, both home and abroad, and steer away from both extremes to grasp the wide spectrum of God's plan for humanity. This means praying for the salvation of both Jews and Arabs. Peace for Jerusalem and for the Arab world can only come through faith in the blood shed by Christ Jesus on the cross. Taking this position means we will be misunderstood by both camps. So be it. We will not lean too strongly either way for we know that Christ died for all, the just One for the unjust ones, to bring us to God.

After the attack on New York's World Trade Center on 9/11 everyone became more keenly aware of the Muslim threat. I was flooded with requests from churches to speak about Islam. One day a charity shop in Reading phoned us.

"Do you have such a thing as an Arabic gospel?" queried a staff member.

I answered that I had bilingual Injils and Scriptures in Persian and Urdu as well as some other languages.

"Oh! We have so many Iranians coming into the shop and asking for the Gospel," this person returned eagerly. So Edna and I took a load of literature to the shop and left it there. Ten days later we returned. We noticed two or three Gospels on the counter and asked if anyone had asked for them.

"Yes! We thought you'd brought us enough for a few years," the staff admitted, "but we already need more!"

They told us about an Algerian man who had walked into the shop with his wife. "They were so excited to see the Scriptures in their language! They were secret believers."

How many Muslims who have emigrated to the West have secretly turned to Jesus Christ? Far more than anyone realizes. In fact, more Muslims have come to Christ in the last fourteen years – worldwide – than during the entire

14 centuries of Islamic history![11] I once got an email from someone in Doncaster, England, telling about a man and woman who had sought asylum in the UK several years before. They couldn't read or write English and there was no interpreter, so on every form they were given at immigration they just put a cross. The immigration officer thought they must be Christians, so he took them outside and pointed to a church with a cross.

Inside that church they found a person who spoke their language. That Muslim couple truly found Christ in that church and have since led so many others to the Lord that they now lead a fellowship of Muslim-background believers.

Read some of the titles suggested in the Appendix for other moving conversion stories. But to see greater numbers turning to Christ we need to become bolder in our witness. I'm praying for gracious, loving but militant Christians in the West who are prepared to walk the streets with banners and show that they belong to Jesus Christ. Christians who will take the risk of rejection to reach out to those without Him. The time has come for salt to be salt and light to be light. We have as examples countless believers in other nations who have paid a heavy price for daring to stand for their Lord.

We also need to acknowledge that we are up against a formidable foe, the same adversary that Paul and the disciples wrestled with. We are at war. It is a spiritual war, and it is real.

Let me share an experience that happened at least twenty years ago. I was invited to speak at a Christian luncheon at the social club of an international oil company, based in London. A good friend of mine was an employee and he was

11 As quoted in the CBN news article "With So Many Muslims Finding Christ, Could Islam Fall?" (1 June 2015).

very overt in his Christian life. The title I was asked to speak on was, *Are Demons for Real?* I accepted the invitation.

On the appointed day I drove my very old, blue Morris Marina to the Reading station car park. Several hundred cars were already there and I left mine in a numbered row of vehicles. I bought my cheap day return ticket and within a short time I was in London.

Inside the high rise building belonging to the oil company I was greeted by my friend and conducted to the meeting room. Forty or more men and women had arrived for the luncheon. My friend introduced me around and it was all systems go. I began by reading aloud two events in Scripture where Jesus delivered individuals from demons and then went into my message, using personal experiences from my own life and work among British people at large, especially those in the military.

I also recounted a few incidents from Borneo. One time when I was with three Chinese brothers, sharing a ministry to a large number of people in a longhouse, we were called to help a woman who was known to be under the influence of demons. She lived in a small wooden house outside the longhouse.

When we entered she just stared at us, then began smirking, laughing, and speaking what seemed to be gibberish. As we started to pray she flung herself on the floor and writhed like a snake, spitting and hissing. We prayed more, read many Scriptures, and commanded the evil spirit controlling her to depart. Nothing happened.

We were dripping with perspiration for the climate was very hot and humid, and there was no electricity for fans or other mod cons. After a couple of hours a man appeared who had just arrived in the village. He overheard us seeking to set the woman free and entered the room, saying "Hush, hush, hush." He then began to speak quietly in another language but with authority, looking directly at the woman.

She scowled at him and became very agitated. Suddenly each of the spirits who controlled her began to leave, one after another, with noise and abhorrent smells, until she was at peace, sitting up and smiling. We then joined our companion in gently laying our hands upon this lady to pray that the vacancy within her would be filled with the Holy Spirit.

Who was the believer and what language did he speak when he commanded those evil spirits to depart? We asked him and he told us that he had had a small government job for many years, but gave it up so that he could share the good news of God to those who were without Him. In effect he was a tribal missionary. The language he spoke was not an earthly one like English or Chinese, but heavenly. Some call this speaking in tongues. It was something quite new to me and I won't go into the how or when or why of it here. But to me it was a "God moment" – the giver of spiritual gifts had brought that brother into the village at that specific moment in order to manifest His grace and power.

Later, I learned that the same woman we prayed for became an evangelist herself, travelling extensively into the interior to share her testimony and preach the Word of God. Such was the power of her transformation.

Following my talk to the oil company employees in London I fielded a lively question and answer period. The time passed quickly with excellent and thought-provoking interaction. I was glad that I had accepted the invitation to speak about this often-neglected subject. Most people, even

Christians, dismiss the idea of Satan's envoys at work in our modern world.

My return to Reading was uneventful... that is, until the moment I walked into the car park. I stopped in my tracks in front of what remained of my old blue car, gasping in shock. The vehicle was completely crushed. All the other cars parked around me were totally untouched; only mine looked like it had been targeted for destruction. Feeling numb, I located the car attendant and asked what had happened.

"Oh, so you'll be the man who owns the car then," the man exclaimed in a heavy southern Irish accent. "Well, I tell yer now, I never seen nothing like it in all me life, so I haven't! 'Twas a big bull, broke loose from the abattoir half a mile away from here. Would ya happen to know it? Sure and if that bull didn't run away from there through the traffic, wid all the cattlemen chasin' after it, all the time shoutin' warnings to people to get out o' the way!

"Well, the creature then decided to turn and gallop up Station Hill. And didn't he then jump the barrier into this very car park? Up and down the rows of cars he ran, those cattlemen doin' their best to catch him. But ye know, it was as if that bull were lookin' for your car only! And when he saw it, he jumped upon it he did, crushing it flat."

The attendant shook his head in wonder. I asked him what time of the day this occurred. He named the exact hour that I was speaking in London about the reality of demons.

I will not bore you with details about the long period of time it took to sort out who was to blame for the damage. The insurance company eventually came up with a pittance that did not approach the amount we needed to replace our car. However, the incident was carried in all the local papers and the news spread. In God's great mercy, a Christian couple who visited us actually bought us a new vehicle! It goes to prove the enemy's power may be great, but our Father's power and provision is greater still. He takes care of His own.

Edna and I have been careful never to jump to conclusions about demons. Some Christians go overboard and declare that a person has a demon if they have a nervous twitch in their face. Or if they walk with a limp they have a "spirit of disability". I could share other examples of such nonsense. However, there have been occasions when we have both been given discernment about a certain individual without speaking to that person.

On one such occasion we were in a congregation worshipping and enjoying the ministry of the Word, but not realizing that both of us at the same time were discerning something unpleasant about a person who was there, but who we scarcely knew at all. Upon reaching home after the service, I asked Edna if she had been blessed by the Word that was preached so faithfully. She said she had, but felt sure the Lord had given her discernment about a man sitting two rows in front of us and to the left. Without her giving me his name, I told her who it was and added that I had discerned that he had an unclean spirit.

We agreed that it was right to be transparent and go to the minister to share what we had discerned. We did this but he could not accept it. In fact, he was severe with us and said we were acting self-righteously. We left his house heavy-hearted.

A few days later I was leading a night of prayer in a rural home a few miles from town. There were ten of us on our knees, seeking God's mercy upon Britain and asking Him to turn us as a nation from sin and uncleanness to repentance and righteousness. Suddenly, just past the midnight hour, we heard a knock and ringing of the front door bell. I rose and went to the door and was somewhat taken aback to see standing before me the man that we had spoken to the minister about. The pastor had told him where I was and urged him to go to the prayer meeting.

I was wondering, of course, if the minister had actually come to realize that this man had a problem. I invited him in and asked him to remove his shoes since we were seeking the Lord for His mercy on Britain, and to our prayer group this was holy ground. He took them off, came into the room, and sat down in a chair, refusing to kneel like the rest of us.

A silence fell as we waited upon God's presence, then I began to worship the Lord and give Him thanks for sending His beloved Son into the world – Jesus, Lord of all.

Immediately our visitor shouted out, "He is not Lord!"

That was enough. I was up on my feet, rebuking the unclean spirit, and the man began to spit, curse, and cry, "We will kill you!"

I quoted the verse, "the one who is in you is greater than the one who is in the world" (1 John 4:4). The words sent him roaring and running out of the house in his bare feet, into a wood nearby. We found a torch and went searching for him, to no avail, though we could still hear him screaming. I decided I should ring the minister, even though it was past midnight. He listened and said we must pray, admitting that he had sent the man to the prayer meeting in the hope that it would help him.

He finally turned up at dawn at the minister's house,

where he was given time to wash, drink fluids, and eat before going to a bed there to sleep. The pastor called a special private meeting of his elders and deacons, inviting the troubled man and myself.

I will not go into a lengthy description of what happened, but the unclean spirit within the man loudly manifested itself to a depth that shocked most who were there. I was not surprised because God had already revealed to me that he had the spirit of sodomy. However, the man wept and cried out to the Lord for mercy and he was delivered, completely set free, and filled with the Holy Spirit.

I rarely exercise a prophetic word, but on this occasion I heard myself saying that within a year this man (who was very overweight) would lose eight stones in weight. He would also marry a godly woman and have children in the following years. That prophecy was fulfilled. He met Edna and me in a supermarket about a year later and hugged us both.

* * *

People often ask us, "When will you retire?" Our reply is, "When we expire!" We spend a lot of our time writing letters of encouragement to workers in many parts of the world. Evangelism continues to be part of our lifestyle, and we are often on the road, responding to invitations to speak at churches, chapels, and conferences in the United Kingdom and Ireland. I have also been privileged to visit a few of the Muslim-background believers mentioned in this book. Edna and I want to do all that we can to raise prayer and financial support to those who are now serving effectively as evangelists in Muslim-dominant countries – often at risk of their lives. Earlier, I mentioned a visit to "Vincent" and his team in Guinea. His ministry requires support which is not available in his homeland. The Singapore-based HIS Mission has been very generous in helping to advance Vincent's work, as well as David's, whose story was also told.

Daniel and Hany Kebede, members of St Matthew's Church in Addis Ababa, took the mantle of David's ministry in Ethiopia after he was martyred, and lovingly cared for the many widows and children of other martyrs in the Saris Christian Centre. Besides providing accommodation, small income-generating projects were started to sustain the women so they would not be tempted by desperation to return to Islam. Not one of them has.

I will share just one poignant story to give you an idea of their plight. Two of the widows had gone to the open market for vegetables. The day was very hot and the place was noisy and dusty, jammed with other women. Noticing a young woman leaning against a tree and looking very ill, the women went over to her to ask questions and offer help.

The young woman was pregnant and had been walking for three weeks with almost nothing to eat. She said that her husband had caught her listening to a Christian radio programme. He beat her and asked if she was a believer in Jesus. When she confessed that she was, he threw her out of the house and went to the mosque to divorce her. She had only the clothes she stood in plus a couple of plastic bags.

The two widows took her to the Saris Centre, but she was so ill that Daniel rang me in England to tell me of her condition and the need for hospitalization. I asked him how much money was in the emergency fund. He said there was nearly US$1,000 so I advised him to take her quickly to the Korean Christian Hospital. He did this and later rang again to say the woman was five months pregnant but the baby in her womb had been dead for two months. They needed to perform a caesarean section but more money was needed, with some extra for recuperation. I instructed him to tell the doctors to go ahead and I would send the balance. Then I got in touch with HIS Mission in Singapore, and Revd Jason Foo and his board. They immediately responded with compassion and sent US$2,000. Christians were alerted to pray, and by God's grace the woman's life was saved and she fully recovered. But that is not the end of the story!

The news of her situation reached her father, who lived in a distant village. He travelled to where she was and upon their meeting she wept, saying she felt ashamed she had not informed him of her circumstances. Knowing he was a Muslim and highly respected, however, she had not wanted to bring shame upon the family.

"You have not brought us any shame," her father responded, then added this telling comment: "There is no compassion in Islam to compare with Christian compassion."

Soon afterwards he and his family of ten children became Christians, and they were all baptized. For safety's sake they took refuge in a European country and now enjoy worship with Christians of different nationalities.

As the premises for Saris Christian Centre became inadequate we rented an old wooden house with a corrugated tin roof since there was no other suitable building. We were able to resettle about twenty of the widows in European countries but others took their place. We are now trusting our Father God to provide sufficient funds to build a replacement centre, with ample space for worship and accommodation. The local bishop and pastor are giving their full support, and we have received more than half of the total needed from Singaporean Christians, with HIS Mission serving as the conduit.

There is no shortage of practical ways that we can advance God's kingdom. For some years we sent consignments of Arabic Scriptures to a Lebanese couple who work and witness among Muslim communities in South Africa. These Scriptures were faithfully sown, and the result has been a number of converts. One man had been a very devout Muslim trained by Sheikh Rahman, the blind sheikh behind the bombing of the World Trade Center in New York. He became a university lecturer. One day he declared that the Quran had no divine origin, and was immediately sacked, attacked, and shot by his own father. God delivered him from death and he was taken in by our friends. He continues to witness, preach, and teach the truth of Jesus Christ.

As Muslim immigrants continue to pour into the West we have access to people who have had little or no previous exposure to the gospel. What an opportunity! On a visit to Australia, Edna and I were made aware of the potential for reaching out to huge immigrant areas in the cities. One Sunday I was invited to speak at a large gathering of people of all ages. I gave many examples of how God was working in various and marvellous ways among Muslims. As soon as I gave the benediction a lady with her daughter approached me and said, "You are meant to be here today for only you can help my daughter and me."

This Christian mother, a former Muslim, related how the Australian authorities had rejected her appeal for residency, not accepting that she and her daughter fled Iran because of the suffocating dictatorial demands and cruelty of her husband. The abuse was largely because they were believers in Jesus Christ.

"This week they are making the final decision. Oh, please help us!" she cried. "God has brought you here today. I know it."

There was something special about this dear lady with her beautiful daughter, and I had an inner witness by the Holy Spirit that I must act immediately. I wrote to the adjudicator in my own hand, stressing that he should consider that if he sent this mother and young daughter back to Iran he would be sentencing the girl to an immediate marriage, very probably to a man twice her age, allowing her no freedom or future. The wife would also become, in effect, a slave, when he married another woman. News came through to us soon after that both mother and daughter were granted permission to stay in Australia. Although we didn't see them again, our hearts rejoice.

When we returned home we sent 800 kilos of Arabic, Syriac, Iranian, and Urdu Scriptures to Australia for ministry to multinational Muslim residents and university students. Besides churches, there are two long-established "Friendship Centres" and a new Iraqi Arabic Bible School employed in this work. Friends of ours have done an effective ministry among hundreds of Muslims through face to face contact, visitation to many in immigration detention centres, and through Bible correspondence courses and teaching. Goodly numbers have come to faith in Jesus as the Son of God and Saviour.

In 2015 I accepted an invitation by the Christian Military Fellowship of Singapore to be the guest speaker at their 45th Anniversary in March. It was held in the

Temasek Club, which was formerly the Sandes Soldiers' and Airmen's Home where Edna and I had once served. I felt quite emotional touring the premises and grounds, taking photos and recalling different events that brought many to the saving knowledge of our Lord Jesus Christ. The dinner was held inside a beautiful restaurant which had once been the cafeteria for thousands of soldiers during 1949 to 1976.

I had handed the Sandes home over to the Singapore government in January 1976 for one dollar. The property is now worth tens of millions and will be demolished in 2016 to make way for a big development scheme.

Pastor Jason Foo, whom I've mentioned before as a dear friend of long standing and founder and director of HIS Mission, was a constant companion and help during those two weeks in Singapore as I spoke at twenty-two meetings and interfaced with many individuals. One surprise and delight was meeting Lawrence and Susan Tong. When he was ten years old Lawrence came to our Chinese boys and girls club. He attended for nearly two years and did a lot of swimming with our son Mark before he was forbidden to go to the club by his Buddhist parents, who were alarmed by his keen interest in Jesus and the stories of the Bible. Today Lawrence is the International Director of Operation Mobilisation, a mission that works in over 115 countries. The seeds planted in his childhood matured and resulted in fruit beyond all expectation.

There are more open doors than closed doors in the world today. No country can be totally closed. Even though millions of dollars are being spent to jam Christian broadcasts, it simply can't be done. There's a crack in the foundations of Islam. In the deserts and in the mountains, men and women and children are coming to the Lord.

In closing, I would like to recount an incident that took place back when I was a boy of nine or ten, and being treated for TB. I'd been released from hospital but still wasn't allowed to go to school or play with other children.

One day I went to the park, where a policeman spotted me. "Boy, come here!" he called. "Why aren't you in school?"

"I've got TB and I've just come out of hospital. I'm not allowed to mix with other children."

He nodded. "Well, you stand right here, because the king is coming by."

"*King George?*" I gasped.

"Yes. He'll be passing in just a few minutes."

Sure enough, a shiny black car appeared on the road as we watched. I jumped up and down, shouting and waving while the policeman saluted.

The car slowed down and I looked right into the eyes of King George VI.

"You run home now and tell everyone you saw the king in Berkeley Avenue," the policeman grinned.

I needed no urging. I rushed home and burst through the door, shouting to my mother that I'd seen the king. She frowned, told me to stop lying, and sent me up to my attic bedroom.

Of course when the local newspaper came two days later I was absolved.

"Tommy, come here!" she called. "You did see King George! The A4 artery was obstructed so he had to take a detour through Berkeley Avenue. I'm sorry," she added, giving me a few pennies by way of apology.

The excitement of that long-ago encounter has never

diminished. Yet I was only a boy, and he was only a king that is now long gone.

Now I look forward with anticipation to a far more wonderful event. *The King of kings is coming back to this earth!* Every eye will see him. My eyes will meet his. And then I want to embrace my King as He embraced me as a desperate teenager so long ago, changing my life for all time.

Edna and I are almost eighty years old as of this writing. We have some physical limitations, yet we can truthfully say we still love each other deeply and are so grateful that God drew us together to serve him and each other. When He comes for us I pray that I will be found faithful to whatever "mission impossible" God assigns. What an incredible privilege to know that our King is able to work out His plan and purpose through even the least of us, as long as we are willing to trust Him. And that's the underlying message of this book.

I commit to you the words of Archbishop Oscar Romero, who was martyred in El Salvador in 1980 for his stand against human rights abuses and the persecution of the church:

> We accomplish in our lifetime only a tiny fraction of the magnificent enterprise that is God's work. Nothing we do is complete. No statement says all that could be said. No prayer fully expresses our faith. No programme accomplishes the Church's mission. No set of goals and objectives includes everything.
>
> This is what we are about. We plant the seeds that one day will grow. We water seeds already planted with our prayers, knowing that they hold future promise. We lay foundations that will need further development. We provide yeast that produces effects

far beyond our capabilities.

We cannot do everything, and there is a sense of liberation in realising that. This enables us to do something, and to do it very well. It may be incomplete, but it is a beginning, a step along the way, an opportunity for the Lord's grace to enter and do the rest. We may never see the end results, but that is the difference between the master builder and the worker.

We are the workers – not the Master Builder; ministers, not Messiahs; we are the prophets of a future not our own.

Amen.

RECOMMENDED BOOKS AND OTHER RESOURCES

Hopefully Tom Hamblin's story has inspired you with the possibility of sharing God's good news with Muslims, both in your own community and in other countries. The material below should inspire you even more. We also include a list of some of the great multi-language media available to you and the new friends you make – plus exciting ministries to support.

Asterisked authors below have written other books worth reading.

Bell, Steven David. *Friendship First, the Manual: Ordinary Christians Discussing Good News with Ordinary Muslims*. Friendship First Publications, 2003.

Caner, Ergun and Emir Fethi Caner. *Unveiling Islam: An Insider's Look at Muslim Life and Beliefs*. Kregel Publications, 2009.

Doyle, Tom. *Dreams and Visions: Is Jesus Awakening the Muslim World?* Thomas Nelson, 2012.

Eedle, Arthur. *Shiraz Meets Jesus*. LULU, 2014.

Fazal, Naeem. *Ex-Muslim: How One Daring Prayer to Jesus Changed a Life Forever*. Thomas Nelson, 2014.

Gabriel, Mark A.* *Islam and Terrorism: What the Quran Really Teaches about Christianity, Violence and the Goals of the Islamic Jihad*. Charisma House, 2002.

Garrison, David. *A Wind in the House of Islam: How God is Drawing Muslims Around the World to Faith in Jesus Christ*. Wigtake Resources LLC, 2014.

RECOMMENDED BOOKS AND OTHER RESOURCES

Gaudeul, Jean-Marie. *Called from Islam to Christ: Why Muslims Become Christians*. Monarch Books, 1999.

Geisler, Norman and Abdul Saleeb. *Answering Islam: The Crescent in Light of the Cross*. Baker Books, 2002.

Goldsmith, Martin.* *Beyond Beards & Burqas; Connecting with Muslims*. Intervarsity Press, 2009.

Goode, Reema. *Which None Can Shut: Remarkable True Stories of God's Miraculous Work in the Muslim World*. Tyndale Momentum, 2010.

Gulshan, Esther. *The Torn Veil: The Gulshan Esther Story*. CLC Publications, 2010.

Maurer, Andreas. *Ask Your Muslim Friend: An Introduction to Islam and a Christian's Guide for Interaction with Muslims*. Zulon Press, 2011.

Pawson, David. *The Challenge of Islam to Christians*. Hodder & Stoughton, 2003.

Quereshi, Nabeel. *Seeking Allah, Finding Jesus: A Devout Muslim Encounters Christianity*. Zondervan, 2014.

Safa, Reza F. *Inside Islam; A Former Radical Shiite Muslim Speaks Out*. Frontline, 1996.

Sasson, Jean.* *Princess: True story of life behind the veil in Saudi Arabia* (Princess Trilogy). Windsor-Brooke Books, 2010.

Sheikh, Bilquis and Richard Schneider. *I Dared to Call Him Father: The Miraculous Story of a Muslim Woman's Encounter with God*. Chosen Books, 2003.

Sookhdeo, Patrick.* *The Essential Guide for Helping Refugees*. Isaac Publishing, 2014.

Steer, Malcolm. *A Christian's Evangelistic Pocket Guide to Islam*. Christian Focus, 2004.

Thompson, Andrew. *Christianity in the UAE: Culture and Heritage*. Motivate Publishing, 2011.

Trousdale, Jerry. *Miraculous Movements: How Hundreds of Thousands of Muslims Are Falling in Love with Jesus*. Thomas Nelson, 2012.

Further helpful media for reaching out to Muslims

About Islam, for Christians

Answering Islam: www.answering-islam.org

Christian Answers: www.christiananswers.net/islam.html

Message for Muslims: http://www.message4muslims.org.uk/

Apologetics, for Muslims seeking truth (in English, Arabic and other languages)

www.answeringmuslims.com

www.debate.org.uk

www.word-of-hope.net

www.Jesus-Islam.org

www.answering-islam.org (25 languages)

http://isaalmasih.net/ (6 languages)

www.the-good-way.com (11 languages)

www.alnour.com/ (Arabic)

www.maarifa.org (Arabic)

http://www.sada-e-haq.com/ (Urdu)

http://www.noor-ul-huda.com/ (Urdu)

Christian websites for Turkish friends

http://incil.com

http://incilturk.com

http://isamesih.com

www.kampusweb.com

www.kutsalkitap.org

http://mujde.org

http://yeniyasam.com

RECOMMENDED BOOKS AND OTHER RESOURCES

Bibles and Christian media sources

Arabic Bible Outreach Ministry: www.arabicbible.com
Online Bible and free materials in Arabic available from other ministries.

Audioscriptures.org: www.audioscriptures.org
Listen to the New Testament in dozens of languages.

Bible League:
http://www.bibleleague.org/resources/bible-download/
Free Bible downloads in many languages.

Bible Society: www.biblesociety.org/
Use this link to find the Bible Society in your country. The biggest Bible translator, publisher and distributor in the world.

Call of Hope: www.call-of-hope.com
Literature, magazine, radio programmes, and stories in English and Arabic.

International Bible Society (Biblica): www.ibs-mena.com/
Bilingual Bibles such as Arabic/English and French/Arabic; downloadable audio Arabic Bible.

Kitab: www.kitab.org.uk
Multimedia, multi-language resources, including literature in minority languages of the Muslim world.

Living Word: http://livingwordbc.org/FarsiBibleNew.asp
Farsi New Testament download.

Multi-Language Media: www.multilanguage.com/ara/Default.htm

No Frontiers (multi-language): www.nofrontiers.org

Pamir Productions: www.sadayezindagi.com
Evangelistic material, books, songs, Scriptures, audio and video for Afghans in Dari and Pashtu.

Persian World Outreach: http://www.persianwo.org/books.htm

Urdu Geo Version Bible download:
http://www.urdugeoversion.com/

Urdu and English tracts: www.openbookministries.org

NOTE: The Bible Society and International Bible Society and Amazon in many countries also sell Arabic Bibles, New Testaments, and audiocassettes.

Correspondence or DVD courses and Bible studies
For Muslims:

The Alif Project: http://www.awm-pioneers.org/the-alif-course/
An exciting video-based course designed by Arab believers to enable
Muslim friends to walk on the journey to faith in Christ.

Bible Outreach Ministry:
http://www.arabicbible.com/bible-course.html
Free Bible studies in Arabic, English, French, and Turkish.

Voice of Preaching the Gospel: www.vopg.org
Free Bible correspondence course.

Word of Life (in English): www.word.org.uk/course
Twenty lessons that introduce a Muslim to the beliefs of those who
follow Isa Al-Masih, referencing both the Bible and Quran.

For Christians:

Bridges: www.crescentproject.org
Six-week DVD-based course by Crescent Projects about Islam and
how Christians can relate to Muslims. Other guides also offered.

Facing the Challenge: www.facingthechallenge.org/quotes.php
Free download of this and other courses, including "What Muslims
Believe".

Orientdienst: https://www.orientdienst.de/muslime/minikurs/
Free online mini-course about Islam in German.

Pioneers: www.encounteringislam.org
"Encountering the World of Islam" book and twelve-week course,
used worldwide.

Seminar about Islam:
http://www.ministeringtomuslims.com/EnglishPages/seminar.html
Free three-part online seminar in English or Italian.

Sharing Lives: www.sharinglives.eu
Excellent five-lesson course taught onsite at a church or group's
invitation. Website also has a helpful blog about Islam, particularly
in Europe.

RECOMMENDED BOOKS AND OTHER RESOURCES

DVDs, videos

Arabian Dawn: https://vimeo.com/45831552
The testimony of a believer from Saudi Arabia.

Arabic language videos: www.christianvideos.org/arabicvideo.html

A Muslim Journey to Hope (Arabic):
www.muslimjourneytohope.com
True stories from individuals. Also three free downloadable books.

Dreams and Visions: http://www.dreamsandvisions.com
Stories of Muslims coming to Christ, viewable online in Arabic,
French or English.

Eden Communications (multi-language):
www.christiananswers.net/catalog/translations.html

Indigitech: http://www.indigitube.tv/?s=muslim
Multi-language video, audio, literature resources.

More Than Dreams: www.visionvideo.com
DVD with dramatic stories of Muslims meeting Christ in five
countries; several languages.

The Life of Jesus: http://www.jesusfilmstore.com/
Special DVD editions of Jesus film in Middle Eastern or Horn of
Africa languages, or watch the film online:
http://www.jesusfilm.org/film-and-media/watch-the-film

Radio and TV

Al Hayat (Life) TV (Arabic): www.alhayat.tv/

Aramaic Broadcasting Network:
http://www.tct.tv/watch-tct/watch-live/abn

Arab Vision: www.arabvision.org

Miracle Channel: Christian Satellite TV for the Arab World:
www.academia.edu/2580453/Miracle_Channel_Christian_
Satellite_TV_for_the_Arab_World

Reach Beyond (formerly HCJB Global): https://reachbeyond.org/

Sat7: www.sat7.org

TBN (Trinity Broadcasting Network):
www.tbn.org/watch-us/broadcasts-on-worldwide-satellite

Other useful websites and key ministries

Arab World Media (AWM): www.awm.org
AWM, a ministry of Pioneers, has a vision "to see mature,
multiplying churches among all Muslim peoples of the Arab world".

Asdika (Friends) Network: www.toxethtab.org.uk/
"Ordinary Christians sharing Good News with ordinary Muslims".

Barnabas Fund: https://barnabasfund.org
Many excellent projects and resources, aiming the majority of its aid
to Christians living in Muslim environments.

Christian Solidarity Worldwide: www.cswusa.org/
Serves the persecuted Christian Church through advocacy, aid and
prayer.

Crescent Project: www.crescentproject.org/
"To inspire, equip and serve the Church to reach Muslims with the
Gospel of Christ for the Glory of God". Practical training.

Directory of Arabic Christian Churches, seminaries, and other
organizations in a number of countries:
www.arabicbible.com/directories/org.htm

Fellowship of Faith for the Muslims: www.ffmna.org
To understand, pray for, and relate God's love to Muslims effectively.

Frontiers: www.frontiers.org/
Reaches out to Muslims and helps others to do so in short- and long-
term teams.

Middle East Christian Outreach (MECO): www.aboutmeco.org
Partners in mission with Middle East Christians. Among the useful
resources on the website is "Engaging with Muslims – A 10 Point
Guide".
NOTE: The Hamblins established a special fund with MECO,
specifically to equip sowers with Arabic and Persian Scriptures.
Contributions can be sent designated for this "Seeds to Sowers"
project to MECO-LIT, PO Box 40793, Larnaca, Cyprus or to their
offices in the USA, Australia, New Zealand, South Africa or the
UK.

Ministering to Muslims: www.ministeringtomuslims.com
Resources for those who want to understand Islam and share their
faith with Muslims.

OM International: www.om.org
Sends a large number of workers to the Muslim world and
distributes literature where most needed. Gifts can be sent to the
OM office in your country, designated for multi-language Scripture
via OM-MENA (Middle East/North Africa).

Open Doors: www.opendoors.org/
Delivers Scriptures to Christians in difficult places.

Praying for All Muslims: www.ffm.org.uk/
FM is an international fellowship of Christians who have an interest
in the Muslim world. Sends news alerts about issues worldwide.

Reach Across: http://uk.reachacross.net
Sharing the gospel with Muslims and encouraging them to become
devoted followers of Jesus Christ in self-sustaining and reproducing
fellowships.

Reaching the Nations Among Us:
http://reachingthenationsamongus.org/
Lots of excellent resources and links to other sites.

Saudi Advocacy Network: http://lovesaudis.com/
Prayer resources and videos, outreach training, and many helpful
links to other information.

The 30-days Prayer Network: www.30-days.net
Excellent guide to praying for Muslims, particularly during
Ramadan each year.

If you enjoyed this book, you might also enjoy:

YOU'VE GOT LIBYA

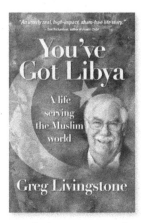

Born out of wedlock, unwanted at birth, how did Greg Livingstone become a pioneer in missions to unreached Muslim peoples? This delightful account, full of compelling humour, strange experiences, and self-deprecating honesty, is a page-turning tour de force. Greg's burden for the millions of Muslims who had no opportunity to hear the gospel led to the launching of Frontiers, a mission agency focusing exclusively on church planting amongst Muslim communities.

"Get more than one copy, so you can pass it on."
– **George Verwer,** Operation Mobilisation

"Highly readable, with plenty of humour and devastating honesty."
– **Colin Chapman,** author of *Whose Promised Land?*

"A hard book to put down!"
– **Phil Parshall,** SIM

ISBN: 978 0 85721 519 2 | e-ISBN: 978 0 85721 520 8

www.lionhudson.com